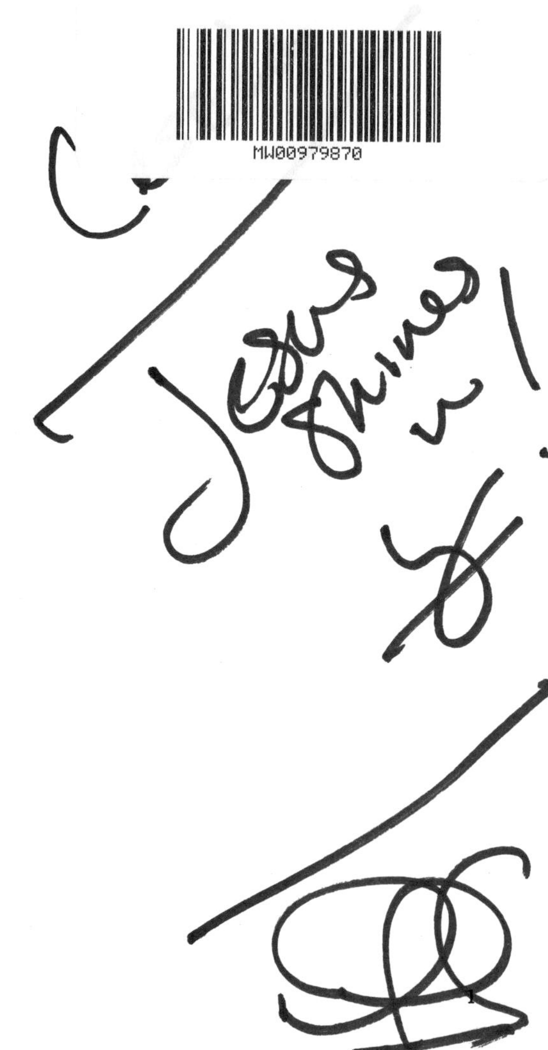

HO:PE AM

A DAILY WAKE UP CALL FOR YOUR HEART

DEAN CURRY

Hope A.M.

Cover design by John Kelley

Printed in the United States of America

ISBN: 978-0692816813

First Edition

INTRODUCTION

There is something in here for YOU.
This whole collection has been formed with you in mind.

Because you are valuable.
Because you are essential.
Because you were created for maximum impact.
Because you crave to be a giver and receiver of HOPE.

Please consider this small devotional a daily deposit in your "hope account."
Let it be a coach when you need a tip on how to get better.
Allow it to be a counselor when you are confused.
Make it a cheerleader when you need to get pumped up.

It will never take more than a few seconds of your day to take in,
And I believe it will add years of fulfillment to your life.
Read it, ponder it, live it, share it.
It was with YOU in mind that I wrote it.

Positively,

HOPE FOR

JANUARY

IN THE BEGINNING

"In the beginning God created the heavens and the earth."
Genesis 1:1

Each new year—in fact, each new day—brings new opportunity for new beginnings. At the very core of each one is God. Whatever you are starting this year, wherever you are starting this year, put Him in the middle of it by offering your plans in prayer. Don't ask God to bless your plans. Instead, ask Him what His plans are, and get behind them.

YOUR NAME HERE

"Salmon was the father of Boaz (whose mother was Rahab)."
Matthew 1:5a

The New Testament portion of the Bible begins with the lineage of Jesus—an ancestry significantly marked by scandalous people who behaved scurrilously. Among these, none was more notorious than Rahab, a prostitute. Whatever is in your past, let it be the past. And know that Jesus can take even the most difficult history and turn it into His story. Need an example? Read the rest of Rahab's story (Joshua 2-6; Hebrews 11:31; James 2:25).

ONE DAY

"Then Jesus said to them, 'The Son of Man is Lord of the Sabbath.'"

Luke 6:5 (NIV)

The Sabbath is one day each week set aside to recharge your batteries spiritually. Don't let religion box you in with guilt and shame. Don't let the momentum of life lock you out by making every day just like the others. Find other Jesus people and welcome Jesus into the center of your day.

JANUARY 4

NEW VISION

"Jesus said to them, 'It is not the healthy who need a doctor, but the sick. I have not come to call the righteous, but sinners.'"
Mark 2:17 (NIV)

For this new year, I hope we ask for "new eyes." Eyes that see people not through a lens of judgment or condemnation, but with compassion. Eyes that see what people are capable of and not just what they have already done. Let's make an effort today to be looking for those who need Jesus—and then treat them with His healing love.

REMEMBER

"So Moses said to the people, 'This is a day to remember forever—the day you left Egypt, the place of your slavery. Today the Lord has brought you out by the mighty power of His hand.'"
Exodus 13:3

There is a lot in our past we would like to forget, but let's not ever forget the deliverance we have received in Jesus. Mark those days, remember those days, and be thankful for those days. Who we are today is a result of what we were delivered from yesterday, and a tribute to the One who delivered us.

JANUARY 6

INVESTMENT

"When Joshua was an old man, the Lord said to him, 'You are growing old, and much land remains to be conquered.'"
Joshua 13:1

Whenever we think of the future, we need to be thinking of investing in other people. As the saying goes, "any plan that is from God is too big for one generation to accomplish." Today I will invest in someone coming behind me so they can conquer new lands. What land lies ahead of you, and who are you preparing to partner with you in conquering it?

SURVIVAL BASICS

"I am the bread of life. Your ancestors ate the manna in the wilderness, yet they died. But here is the bread that comes down from heaven, which anyone may eat and not die."
John 6:48-50 (NIV)

There are some essentials we need for physical survival. Bread and water are a couple of the basics. There's another essential we need for spiritual survival. That spiritual basic is Jesus. He is the bread of life. He sustains not just your body, but your soul. Not just your life here on earth, but your life for eternity. Today, use the name of Jesus two or three times. Share with someone what He has meant to you.

JANUARY 8

BETRAYAL

"Now while they were staying in Galilee, Jesus said to them, 'The Son of Man is about to be betrayed into the hands of men.'"
Matthew 17:22 (NKJV)

Betrayal hurts, doesn't it? Carrying bitterness for every betrayal compounds the hurt even more. Who has betrayed you? Whether the betrayal was recent or some time ago, make it a point today to pray your betrayer's name out loud, and bless and forgive him or her with the words of your mouth. Jesus experienced fatal betrayal from one of His closest companions, and He knew in advance that it would happen. Yet He taught His followers to "Bless those who curse you. Pray for those who hurt you" (Luke 6:28). Live lighter today: choose blessing over bitterness.

ASSIGNMENT

"I have brought you glory on earth by finishing the work you gave me to do."
John 17:4 (NIV)

Jesus had an assignment here on earth and He saw it through to the finish. Remind yourself today that you have an assignment also. Your assignment is in a place, to the people in that place, to reveal God's power and glory to those people in that place. Look for opportunity today to complete your assignment.

JANUARY 10

LORD

"I am the Alpha and the Omega, the First and the Last, the Beginning and the End."
Revelation 22:13

Jesus was more than a philosopher, more than a teacher, more than a social commentator. He was the originator and creator, and He was God in the flesh. Don't make Jesus your guru; make Him the Lord of your life today.

HE IS

"Jesus answered, 'I tell you the truth, before Abraham was even born, I AM!'"
John 8:58

Whatever you're going through, it's not a surprise to Jesus. He has seen it all, walked with people through it all. Don't pretend or imagine He is overwhelmed by your dilemma. Before the ancients were born, He was and is. Trust Him today with your problem.

JANUARY 12

HELP WANTED

"The woman came and knelt before him. 'Lord, help me!' she said."
Matthew 15:25 (NIV)

It's been said that there are only three prayers that really matter: Lord, help me. Lord, teach me. Lord, use me. Never be too proud to pray or ask those two powerful words: "Help me."

CHOSEN

"You did not choose me but I chose you. And I appointed you to go and bear fruit, fruit that will last, so that the Father will give you whatever you ask him in my name."
John 15:16 (NRSV)

You were born for great things. Be encouraged today. If the "fruit" of your life doesn't seem as sweet as you would like it to be, put your roots down in Jesus. You were created for greatness. Walk like a child of God today.

JANUARY 14

TODAY

"Jesus said to him, "I tell you the truth, today you will be with me in paradise.""

Luke 23:43 (NCV)

To my knowledge, the thief who was crucified on the cross next to Jesus had never been to a lecture Jesus gave, was never baptized, had never attended a church. But he recognized who Jesus was, craved the forgiveness Jesus offered, and had the courage to ask for it. Jesus answered with a promise and the word "today." And the moment the forgiven criminal took his last breath on earth, he took his next breath in paradise. It's never too late to ask for and trust in the forgiveness of Jesus.

LESS TRAVELED

"Enter through the narrow gate. For wide is the gate and broad is the road that leads to destruction, and many enter through it."
Matthew 7:13

It's so easy to be average or common. It is the route most taken, the road most traveled. Conversely, to be a follower of Jesus is to take the road less traveled. What is everyone around you doing, including those who don't yet know Jesus? If everybody's doing it, it may not be a Jesus thing. Be uncommon today and make a point of stopping any behavior, thought, or emotion that is common and unworthy of a child of God.

JANUARY 16

FEARLESS

"Do not be afraid of those who kill the body but cannot kill the soul."
Matthew 10:28a (NIV)

Fear has almost become the status quo in our world where headlines regularly feature terrorists, criminals, natural disasters, and others who can hurt us. But Jesus Himself reminds us that what happens in the natural is nothing compared to the significance of the spiritual. Today, put as much energy into protecting your soul as you do into protecting your body. Read God's word. Listen to His Spirit. Pray in Jesus' name. Live fearlessly.

FAITH

"So give me the hill country that the Lord promised me."

Joshua 14:12a

Years before the day he made this statement, Caleb had been a scout in the Promised Land and had seen a territory that he claimed as his promise. Decades passed before he saw it again, this time to claim it. What has Lord promised you that you have not claimed yet? Don't give up and don't give in. Keep asking, keep trusting, and be ready to claim the "hill country" when He is ready to give it.

JANUARY 18

PROMISES

"And she made this vow: 'O Lord of Heaven's Armies, if you will look upon my sorrow and answer my prayer and give me a son, then I will give him back to you.'"

1 Samuel 1:11a

Hannah is known in history as a woman who saw great things happen through her son. His birth was a miracle and his life was a miracle. Whatever you have pledged to God, do your level best to fulfill that promise. On good days and bad days, whatever we say in our tears and in celebration, we should fulfill with faithfulness. Integrity is built by making promises and keeping them.

FREEDOM

"Here is a list of the family leaders and the genealogies of those who came with me from Babylon."
Ezra 8:1a

Sometimes we spend more breath and time talking about the captivity we have fallen into, than we do celebrating all who have walked out of captivity. Think of those you know who are living great lives despite mistakes or circumstances of the past. Think of families you know and love who have walked out of captivity. Today is a day to celebrate redemption and freedom.

JANUARY 20

LEARNING 101

"To learn, you must love discipline;
it is stupid to hate correction."
Proverbs 12:1

Every great person I know runs toward responsibility and receives correction. What hint, critique, or criticism keeps recurring in your life? Perhaps it's time to receive it and learn from it—to use it as a stepping stone and not a stumbling block.

RESCUE

"The Lord replies, 'I have seen violence done to the helpless, and I have heard the groans of the poor. Now I will rise up to rescue them, as they have longed for me to do.'"
Psalm 12:5

Today, say a prayer for those who are suffering around the world: people who have been hurt in famines, floods, and fighting. May God hear their cries as He has throughout the ages.

JANUARY 22

NEVER ALONE

"And I will ask the Father, and he will give you another Advocate, who will never leave you."
John 14:16

You are not just a person of intellect or mind; you are also a person of spirit. If you have Jesus in your heart, you have His Spirit guiding your life. When you face a dilemma today, invite the Holy Spirit to give you wisdom beyond what your own mind can comprehend or calculate.

ONE WAY

"And this is the way to have eternal life—to know you, the only true God, and Jesus Christ, the one you sent to earth."
John 17:3

This prayer Jesus spoke to His Father is still true today. With all of the prosperity and opportunity available to us in our modern world, truly the only thing that matters is that we know Jesus and that we can look forward to heaven. Share with someone today what Jesus has done for you.

CRITICS WELCOME

"Woe to you when everyone speaks well of you."
Luke 6:26a (NIV)

If people are saying discouraging things about you today, you are in good company. In fact, Jesus offers caution to anyone who is not living uncommonly enough to receive some criticism. Jesus received rebuke and rejection. Should we really expect better treatment than He received?

ALL OR NOTHING

"I said to myself, 'Come on, let's try pleasure. Let's look for the "good things" in life.' But I found that this, too, was meaningless."
Ecclesiastes 2:1

Don't spend your time, your thoughts, and your heart on envying those who "have it all." One more time we are reminded that those who "have it all" without Jesus, have nothing at all. Yet those who have Jesus and nothing else...have everything.

PASS IT ON

"Go to the entrance of the Lord's Temple, and give this message to the people: 'O Judah, listen to this message from the Lord! Listen to it, all of you who worship here!'"
Jeremiah 7:2

Don't just be an attender. Be a participant, a believer, and a message-bearer. What do you do with the messages you hear in church? What do listen to during the week? What are you reading? Are you in a small group that talks about life and truth? Find wisdom and receive it, apply it, and give it away to someone else.

REST

"Then Jesus said, 'Come to me, all of you who are weary and carry heavy burdens, and I will give you rest.'"
Matthew 11:28a

Jesus literally invites the tired. To be weary is to lose not only the energy but the joy. So if you are tired, joyless, and have heavy things weighing you down, Jesus is your answer today. Feel free to give the answer of Jesus to all you see in this condition.

JANUARY 28

HOME

"Jesus said to the people who believed in him, 'You are truly my disciples if you remain faithful to my teachings.'"
John 8:31

To abide means to live in. To have an abode means to have a house. If you make your home in the sentences, truths, and words of Jesus, you are His follower. Make your home in who Jesus says you are; in what Jesus says you are born for; in what Jesus says about your past, your present, and your future.

SET FREE

"And you will know the truth,
and the truth will set you free."
John 8:32

These are the words Jesus spoke next after urging his followers to make their home in Him by knowing and following His teachings. When we make our home in Jesus, we know the truth—truth that unlocks every door that stands between us and our destiny.

AT HEART

"Then he turned to his critics and asked, 'Does the law permit good deeds on the Sabbath, or is it a day for doing evil? Is this a day to save life or to destroy it?' But they wouldn't answer him."

Mark 3:4

People who immerse themselves in religion love to focus on strict obedience of the letter of the law, while ignoring the heart of the law and its purpose. Be a follower of Jesus. His heart was that you would maximize every day to do good and to save a life. Look for opportunities to do that today.

MINDSET

"'Listen to me and make up your minds to honor my name,' says the Lord of Heaven's Armies...."
Malachi 2:2a

Determination is one of the main contributors to success. When we set our minds on something, it changes everything. Set your mind today to honor Jesus, to honor His name in your actions, attitudes, and affirmations. Be a light to those around you. Honor is a magnet for greatness.

FEBRUARY

ATTRIBUTION

"Then the Lord said to Moses,
'Pay close attention to this.
I will make you seem like God to Pharaoh.'"
Exodus 7:1a

Sometimes when people see the power of God working through you, they attribute it to you. Never forget to remind people that all the good they see in you is Jesus.

FEBRUARY 2

BASE HIT

"If anyone gives you even a cup of water because you belong to the Messiah, I tell you the truth, that person will surely be rewarded."
Mark 9:41

Sometimes in our big, busy, flashy world, we lose sight of the power of a small gesture done in love. Teresa of Calcutta was the world's greatest proponent of small gestures done in love. Like offering a cup of cold water, or sitting and listening to a friend who is struggling. Today, don't look for home run plays. Instead, look for small opportunities to do something kind in Jesus' name. Get on base today.

THOUGHTS

"For from the heart come evil thoughts, murder, adultery, all sexual immorality, theft, lying, and slander."
Matthew 15:19

Most of us are not nearly as careful as we could be about keeping a tight rein on our thoughts. A thought becomes powerful when we entertain it. That entertaining turns into voicing, and the voicing turns into action. Today, don't just be careful about the power of your words; be careful about the power of your thoughts. Think things that bless others and nourish you.

FEBRUARY 4

LITTLE ONES

"But if you cause one of these little ones who trusts in me to fall into sin, it would be better for you to have a large millstone tied around your neck and be drowned in the depths of the sea."
Matthew 18:6

Today, be thoughtful about habits, sentences, or behaviors that might cause the little people in your world to be confused. Perhaps the most common sin in our age is the sin of destroying innocence. Let's live today as if a seven-year-old is watching every move we make. Because he or she probably is.

COMFORT

"God blesses those who mourn,
for they will be comforted."
Matthew 5:4

Sometimes we forget that it is in our weakness that God works most powerfully (2 Corinthians 12:9). If you are mourning something today, don't hide it. Confess it, pray over it, and let His Spirit lift your spirits.

FEBRUARY 6

RIGHT

"God blesses those who are persecuted for doing right, for the Kingdom of Heaven is theirs."
Matthew 5:10

We may not welcome persecution, but it is inevitable. It's nice to know there is a blessing in it when it is connected to our faith and devotion to Jesus. This world is becoming more and more adversarial to genuine faith, yet blessed is the one who is struggling for all the right reasons.

SO THAT

"'It was not because of his sins or his parents' sins,' Jesus answered. 'This happened so the power of God could be seen in him.'"
John 9:3

I don't believe in karma—that we get what we get because of past mistakes. I believe in grace—that God overlooks our mistakes and covers them with His grace. Don't live today as if every bad thing you are experiencing is because of something that happened in the past. Instead, realize that Jesus takes every event in our lives and redeems it for His glory and His greatness.

INHERITANCE

"Then the King will say to those on his right, 'Come, you who are blessed by my Father, inherit the Kingdom prepared for you from the creation of the world.'"
Matthew 25:34

Every follower of Jesus has a great inheritance waiting for him or her. Sadly, we are often either unaware or uninterested in the inheritance set aside for us. When we live for Jesus and walk away from the distractions and destruction of this world, we are walking toward our inheritance. Live today like a person who knows great things are waiting for you.

FIXED

"You will keep in perfect peace all who trust in you, all whose thoughts are fixed on you!"
Isaiah 26:3

It has long been understood by physiologists that we move in the direction of our dominant thoughts. Here the Scriptures remind us that when our minds are dominated by thoughts of God, peace is the harvest. What is your obsession today? What is your focus? Set your mind on the things of God and peace will be your outcome.

FEBRUARY 10

PEERLESS

"I am leaving you with a gift—peace of mind and heart. And the peace I give is a gift the world cannot give."
John 14:27a

Peace is part of the inheritance for every Jesus follower. Religion cannot offer peace. Financial gain offers only a fleeting version of peace. Health comes and goes. The peace Jesus offers as your inheritance cannot be taken from you. It is something the world does not have and cannot give. Talk to Jesus first thing this morning.

ANTIDOTE

"Do not be anxious about anything, but in every situation, by prayer and petition, with thanksgiving, present your requests to God."
Philippians 4:6 (NIV)

"Do not be anxious about anything" seems like a big challenge. It is the Mount Everest of our thought life. It is so easy to want more and become anxious, to dream for more and become anxious, or to reflect and become anxious. Whether we are looking at the past, the present, or the future, let nothing, nothing be so precious to us that we would not take time in prayer to ask, to be grateful, and to see what God can do. The promise is that God's peace, which exceeds anything we can understand, will guard our hearts and minds (Philippians 4:7).

FEBRUARY 12

WHY INDEED

"The Lord is my light and my salvation—
so why should I be afraid?"
Psalm 27:1a

He is your light because when you cannot see, He helps you to see. He is your salvation because when you were dying in your heart, your mind, and your soul, He rescued you. "Why should I be afraid?" is a rhetorical question. Nothing and no one can dim His light or steal His salvation. Be confident today that whatever darkness you are in, He can light your way and save you from every enemy.

COURAGE

"As soon as I pray, you answer me; you encourage me by giving me strength."
Psalm 138:3

So many Jesus people lack courage. Because they lack courage, they lack adventure. Because they lack adventure, they lack joy. Because they lack joy, they have no strength, for the joy of the Lord is a believer's strength. When you cry out, He will answer you. And when He answers you, He makes you as bold as a lion. Be courageous today. You are a follower of the King of kings.

ALL!

"I can do all things through Christ,
who strengthens me."
Philippians 4:13 (WEB)

When I read this verse, the word "all" is capitalized in my head with exclamation points after it. ALL things! We not only have ability, but we also have authority because we are with the King. His authority and His ability, plus the abilities He gives us as gifts, make every day full of possibilities. Walk today as someone who is paying attention to opportunity and not obstacles. Because you can do ALL things. You don't have to do all things. You're not forced to do all things. But you can do ALL things through Him. Be encouraged today.

LOVE, GOD

"For God has not given us a spirit of fear and timidity, but of power, love, and self-discipline."
2 Timothy 1:7

There are certain things that, if they end up on your doorstep, you know are not from a friend. If you wake up this morning with fear, that is from the enemy, not from the lover of your soul. Power, love, and a sound mind are all gifts that come from a spirit of love. For God is love and He has made Himself clear: He adores you.

FEBRUARY 16

RESCUE

"Many are the afflictions of the righteous, but the Lord delivers him out of them all."
Psalm 34:19 (ESV)

I am so convinced these words are true. God never promises He can or will stop afflictions. Some afflictions are from the enemy, some are results of circumstance, and others are self-inflicted. But the Lord delivers us out of them all. All, all, all! There is no trouble our God cannot drag His children out of. Trust Him, talk to Him, walk with Him today.

SAFE

"Though a thousand fall at your side, though ten thousand are dying around you, these evils will not touch you."
Psalm 91:7

I claim this promise when fear creeps in in the early morning hours or the late hours of the evening. Sometimes we forget that the desires of our heart and the meditations of our mind are things we can give to Jesus. Whatever others around us may be going through, we can be assured He won't lead us into anything that will separate us from Him. Be encouraged today.

AUTHORITY

"You have already been pruned and purified by the message I have given you."
John 15:3

Authority makes our words matter. If a police officer says pull over, we pull over. If a teacher says you passed the test, then you passed the test. Jesus is asserting authority here. He is affirming that the only thing needed for your heart to change is for Him to speak words of healing over you. The next time you are in a place where people are accepting Christ by a simple confession, remember this. All it takes is a word by the right authority.

WHO

"I tell you the truth, those who listen to my message and believe in God who sent me have eternal life. They will never be condemned for their sins, but they have already passed from death into life."
John 5:24

Your destiny is truly set by who you believe. People are giving you signals every day. Green lights, red lights, yellow lights. Go, stop, caution. The signals you believe not only determine your pace but your destiny as well. Jesus tells us here, listen to My message and believe in God who sent Me. Don't trust yourself, the enemy, or the culture. Trust Him today and live.

FEBRUARY 20

WORDS

"And the very words I have spoken to you are spirit and life."
John 6:63b

"Sticks and stones may break my bones but words will never hurt me." This old saying is well worn and familiar to most, but it has never been true. It has always been in error. Spoken words are either life or death. Jesus tells His followers that the words He has spoken are "spirit and life." Read His words today. Meditate on them and hear His voice speaking them to you. Words of life, words of encouragement.

REBIRTH

"Jesus told her,
'I am the resurrection and the life.'"
John 11:25a

Jesus is saying, I am the force that reanimates what was dead. The Bible says we are dead until we claim the life Jesus offers. When we receive Him, Jesus not only brings us back from the dead (resurrection), He also regenerates us and gets us going (life). We are not spiritual zombies; we are spiritual babies. You are a new person. This is a new day. You have new life and new opportunities. Make the most of it today.

FEBRUARY 22

SOURCE

"Yes, I am the vine."
John 15:5a

Jesus is using an agricultural illustration for an agricultural people. He is saying, I am the source. Have you talked to the source today? If you are in need, where do you go? Let Him be your source. Not a television, not a bottle, not a pill, or even a friend. Let Jesus be your source today. Talk to Him, rely on Him, listen to Him, and obey Him.

BRANCHES

"You are the branches."
John 15:5b

Jesus is saying here that we are not designed to be apart from Him, any more than a branch is designed to be apart from the vine. It is not possible for a branch to thrive on its own. By definition, a branch exists and lives because of its connection to the vine. Don't be self-sufficient today. Don't be proud or independent. You are connected to the greatest power in the universe.

FEBRUARY 24

ALWAYS

"Rejoice always."
1 Thessalonians 5:16a (NIV)

This Scripture expects a lot. It asks us to overlook our mood, overlook our circumstances, overlook the time of day, and sometimes overlook the people we are with. It does not ask us to rejoice about everything; it just says to do it always. It gives instruction about timing, not circumstance. It's always a good time to be grateful. It's always a good time to thank God. Try it today regardless of anything and everything else. Always rejoice.

TREASURE

"And now, dear brothers and sisters, one final thing. Fix your thoughts on what is true, and honorable, and right, and pure, and lovely, and admirable."
Philippians 4:8a

It takes a lot of focused energy to look for these qualities. They are rare. Which means they are hard to find. Natural diamonds aren't just lying around everywhere. They are buried deep, and you have to dig like crazy to get to them. So, today, look for what's true. Search for what's honorable. Have an eye for what is right, pure, lovely, and admirable. When you find it, hold it, treasure it, protect it, and be grateful for it.

FEBRUARY 26

RARE

"Think about things that are excellent and worthy of praise."
Philippians 4:8b

If you are looking for something to ponder, don't choose what is common. Think on the rare. Things that are hardest to find are the most valuable. Today, try this: Don't meditate on the qualities that annoy you most about the person sitting across from you. Focus on the one quality that makes him or her exceptional. Talk about it, express thanks for it, and shine a spotlight on it.

UNCOMMON

"Don't use foul or abusive language. Let everything you say be good and helpful, so that your words will be an encouragement to those who hear them."
Ephesians 4:29

We live in a world of opinions, critique, and coarseness. It's all too easy to fall into the flow of that river. But as followers of Jesus, we have our instructions. Not only are we to stop the negative flow, but we are to do what is good, what builds up, and what extends grace. Don't just stop the negative; pump out the positive. Be a source of greatness today. Be a source of the uncommon.

CERTAIN TRUMPET

"Commit everything you do to the Lord. Trust him, and he will help you."
Psalm 37:5

There's an old quote attributed to Theodore Hesburgh of the University of Notre Dame: "You can't blow an uncertain trumpet." In essence, I believe this is what the psalmist is saying here. Commit. Don't be wishy-washy or halfhearted, don't be maybe or if. Be a certain trumpet. Commit your way to Jesus. When you do that, He will act, and He will act miraculously. Look for a miracle. It follows your commitment.

BECAUSE

"What blessings await you when people hate you and exclude you and mock you and curse you as evil because you follow the Son of Man."
Luke 6:22

The key here is the ending: "because you follow the Son of Man." Lots of us draw hatred and animosity because of our own silliness, stupidity, or selfishness. But when we are doing good, being good, and aspiring to good, and still attract evil, Scripture says we are blessed. You are blessed if you can bless those who curse you. You are blessed if you see the best in everyone and yet they still find fault in that. If you still draw fire after being that kind of peacemaker, you are in elite company.

HOPE FOR MARCH

WINNING

"And when you hear of wars and insurrections, don't panic."
Luke 21:9

So often when we think about end times or the days in which we live, we quickly go to fear. But Jesus Himself said, when it comes to changing times, don't be frightened. Revolution requires change, and Jesus is a revolutionary. He revolutionizes the way we think, the way we feel, the way we act. And as He does this, the world revolts against Him. You are in a battle. Don't be frightened. Don't be paralyzed and don't give up. You are winning! You have the general of all generals, the King of all kings as your leader. Be encouraged.

MARCH 2

MISSION

"Now get up and go into the city,
and you will be told what you must do."
Acts 9:6

Go into your city today knowing you will receive instruction when you are where you are meant to be. Jesus has a place for you. Go to that place, be in that place, and He will send instruction just in time. Never too late, never too early, always on time. Listen for it today.

HEARSAY

"'But Lord,' exclaimed Ananias, 'I've heard many people talk about the terrible things this man has done to the believers in Jerusalem!'"
Acts 9:13

Be careful not to listen to the reports of the people around you, but to believe and follow the instruction the Spirit gives you. When you get a whisper from God, no other report matters. Here Ananias is given instruction about a man who would become the leader of the church: the apostle Paul. To some, Paul was just a murderer, just a criminal, just a man on the run. But where the world saw a murderer, God saw a messenger. Believe God's report today; it's reliable.

MARCH 4

INSTRUMENT

"But the Lord said,
'Go, for Saul is my chosen instrument....'"
Acts 9:15a

You, too, are an instrument of the Almighty God. When He picks you up, beautiful music comes out of you. Here the Lord is saying He sees goodness in a man full of darkness. He is telling His people, "This man is My instrument. He belongs to Me for beautiful music." Today, keep in mind that you are His instrument. When you hear beautiful notes coming from you, remember it is the music of the Musician, and not just the instrument.

MESSENGER

"...to take my message to the Gentiles and to kings, as well as to the people of Israel."
Acts 9:15b

Three groups of people are mentioned here: the lost, the powerful, and the godly. Today, look for people from these three groups. Take the name of Jesus to someone who is lost, to someone who is a brother or sister, and to someone in a position of power. The name of Jesus is welcome in any court, in any office, in any classroom, and in any home. People don't want religion, but they do want Jesus. He is the Prince of Peace.

MID-DAY

"About noon..."
Acts 26:13a

I love how the Bible sometimes gives a specific timeline of when things happened. This story begins by telling us it was in the heat of the day, the hungry part of the day, the hustle and bustle of the day. Today, in the middle of your day, I believe God wants to connect with you. You don't have to just meet Him in the morning or at night; you can talk to Him in the middle of your day. Expect Him in the most unexpected places. He loves to surprise you and fill you with wonder. Look for Him today. Wait for Him today. Expect Him today.

SIT

"He sat down,
called the twelve disciples over to him..."
Mark 9:35a

It is well known that in Jesus' time the great teachers or rabbis taught from a seated position while others gathered around them to listen. Let this be a reminder to you to pause today with your people, to take a moment with your students, to gather your children around you and teach them what Jesus has done for you. You are a person of influence. Every day people look to you for nourishment for their heart, mind, and soul. Take a moment today to sit with someone who matters to you.

MARCH 8

AMBITION

"Whoever wants to be first must take last place and be the servant of everyone else."
Mark 9:35b

Ambition and the desire for fame seem to be a part of our "reality TV" culture, where people care more about being famous than what they're famous for. Jesus explains here the inverted pyramid of the Kingdom. If you want to be ambitious, aspire to be a servant. Whenever I talk about or reflect on the topic of serving, I am reminded of Teresa of Calcutta. She was a tiny woman who cast a massive shadow over the poorest city in the world because she served. Her legacy continues to influence the world today.

YOU KNOW

"'But why did you need to search?' he asked. 'Didn't you know that I must be in my Father's house?'"
Luke 2:49

Theologians have wrestled with this statement made by Jesus when He was a child. We read earlier in Jesus' story that Mary treasured in her heart what the angel told her at Jesus' conception and birth. Yet Mary seems not to have calculated that in this instance. What are we not including in our current circumstances about the messages Jesus has given us? Remember who you are today, and who He is. Recall what He has given you and what He has assigned you. Walk like a person with purpose.

MARCH 10

SCATTERED

"But the time is coming—indeed it's here now—when you will be scattered...."
John 16:32a

There's no debate about whether or not persecution will come. When it does, change will arrive with it. The only question is, can you see the hand of God even in the scattering? As the disciples were scattered throughout the known world, the message of Jesus went with them. As change comes in your life, so will the message of Jesus go with you. What the enemy means for evil, God has a way of turning for the best.

ELEVATED

"Therefore, God elevated him to the place of highest honor...."
Philippians 2:9a

Good news! Because of who Jesus was, He was elevated by the Father. Because of who you are in Jesus, He has a promotion for you, too. What makes you think He won't elevate you if the Spirit of His Son lives in you? Everyone who receives Jesus and is full of His Spirit is receiving an inheritance. Good days and bad days come and go, but you can be at ease knowing God elevates us at just the right time.

MARCH 12

RESULTS

"Work hard to show the results of your salvation, obeying God with deep reverence and fear."
Philippians 2:12b

Here the Philippians are being encouraged to work hard to show people the results of what Jesus has done. They do that by living with reverence and appropriate fear of God. What can you and I do today to make space for reverence in our life? Take a moment to think about how you can prune your life so people can see the most and best fruit of Jesus' work in you.

CHANGE

"This change of plans greatly upset Jonah, and he became very angry. So he complained to the Lord about it..." Jonah 4:1-2a

Can you relate to this? God allows or directs a change of plans that does not sync with our expectations, and we become angry. So instead of changing our expectations, we ask God to change His plans. Aren't we silly people, we who want to play the role of creator in our own lives? If a change of plans happens today, trust Him. See if He turns it into a great victory.

MARCH 14

HEART MONITOR

"But Daniel was determined not to defile himself...."
Daniel 1:8a

There are twelve chapters in the book of Daniel full of exploits and prophesies of one of Scripture's most influential figures. And it all happens because this man had a heart so in love with God that he shunned wrong appetites so he could feed his appetite for God instead. The writer of the wisdom books wrote, "Guard your heart above all else" (Proverbs 4:23). Daniel nailed it. How are you doing today?

RELATIONSHIP

"The Lord is more pleased when we do what is right and just than when we offer him sacrifices."
Proverbs 21:3

The key to religion is action and ritual. The key to relationship is love and obedience. When we love Jesus, we obey Him, and when we obey Him, He knows our behavior is from the heart and not just repetition. We are more than just a series of habits. We are heart and soul. Put your heart into something today just because you love Jesus. Don't tell anyone else; just do it for Him.

MARCH 16

STREETS

"Then the angel showed me a river with the water of life, clear as crystal, flowing from the throne of God and of the Lamb. It flowed down the center of the main street."
Revelation 22:1-2a

Where do you live? Do you have an expectation that Jesus and the peace that comes with Him could be flowing down the streets of your neighborhood? Pray today for the homes, apartments, condos, businesses, and people on your block. As I often do where I live, say out loud with expectation, "This place is a Jesus place. This dirt belongs to Jesus."

RESPONSIBILITY

"Moses commanded Joshua, 'Choose some men to go out and fight the army of Amalek for us. Tomorrow, I will stand at the top of the hill, holding the staff of God in my hand.'" Exodus 17:9

I try to ask myself often, What do I have authority over? I have authority over my family. I have a sphere of authority at work. I have authority as a citizen of my city, as a citizen of the United States. I have authority within each of these areas and maybe a few more. When I read Moses' command, I am reminded that wherever I have authority, I also have the responsibility to pray over that place and those people. Moses went above the battle because prayer to the heavens dictates the victory in the battlefield. Today, remember to pray for your family and friends, for your church, for your city, state, country, and brothers and sisters around the world. You have authority and you also have responsibility. Exercise both today.

MARCH 18

REMINDER

"After the victory, the Lord instructed Moses, 'Write this down on a scroll as a permanent reminder, and read it aloud to Joshua….'"
Exodus 17:14a

It's important that we don't just go through victories, but that we savor them. Life is full of battles and when you finish one battle, you are really just in a respite until the next. A respite doesn't give you courage to face the next enemy; only rejoicing and reminding yourself of the victory does. Today, remind yourself. Recollect the times Jesus has blessed you and God has rescued you. As you remember, rejoice. The joy you store up today will be your strength for the next battle.

INHERITANCE

"A wise servant will rule over the master's disgraceful son and will share the inheritance of the master's children."
Proverbs 17:2

Sometimes we have a hard time imagining a positive future because we have had a negative or less than glorious past and heritage. This proverb reminds us that it is faithfulness and honor that lead to a great inheritance, not lineage. Many who have had a great lineage of faith have neglected and rejected it and will have no blessing for their children. But you and I, who might have less than ideal histories, can be heirs to a great spiritual fortune. Look forward today to the fruit of your faithfulness and don't grow weary of doing good.

MARCH 20

TESTING

"Fire tests the purity of silver and gold,
but the Lord tests the heart."
Proverbs 17:3

When fire tests gold it burns away what is called dross, the waste and impurities. This makes the gold soft and more valuable. The same is true when God tests our heart. At first we are tempted to get hard and bitter, but if we let the Holy Spirit do His work, He makes us more soft and precious to those around us, and certainly more prepared for heaven. In times of testing, it's hard to appreciate the experience itself. But as things "cool down," others around you will see the brilliance of your soul.

MOMENTUM

"And the judgment is based on this fact: God's light came into the world, but people loved the darkness more than the light, for their actions were evil." John 3:19

Momentum has a lot of significance. When something gets moving in one direction, it starts building force in that direction. And as we know from science, it tends to continue in that direction unless variables intervene. Sin has a momentum all its own and will propel you long after the initial inclination to sin has passed. This is why we need to be constantly on guard against the momentum of our appetites. The best strategy is to focus on giving momentum to our faith, to our hope, and to real love. When we get up in the morning, often we are thinking of self. But every time we make a decision to stop the momentum of selfishness and to push the momentum of great living, we are building a heritage and a legacy.

MARCH 22

AUTHENTICITY

"What sorrow awaits you teachers of religious law and you Pharisees. Hypocrites! For you are so careful to clean the outside of the cup and the dish, but inside you are filthy—full of greed and self-indulgence!"
Matthew 23:25

In a world preoccupied with external appearance, Jesus people are called to be through-and-through people. Jesus works not from the outside (appearance) in, but from the inside (character) out. People may not initially see the change happening in you, but they will inevitably and eventually see it. The facade of goodness is really intended to keep criticism at bay, while the reality of goodness actually keeps the enemy at bay. Be encouraged today.

TRAVEL ESSENTIALS

"He told them to take nothing for their journey except a walking stick—no food, no traveler's bag, no money. He allowed them to wear sandals but not to take a change of clothes."
Mark 6:8-9

We live in the most opulent culture that has ever existed. The most affluent and perhaps the most indulgent. Jesus gives us instruction from time to time that all we really need are the essentials: the minimum physically and the maximum spiritually. To have a full suitcase and an empty heart does you no good. To have a full heart and an empty suitcase can be a great life. When you find yourself thinking about what you don't have, remind yourself today that the early followers of Jesus practiced going without in their hands because they were full in their hearts. Go and do likewise.

MARCH 24

MOVE ON

"But if any place refuses to welcome you or listen to you, shake its dust from your feet as you leave to show that you have abandoned those people to their fate."

Mark 6:11

The power of our blessing is significant. This passage reminds us there is also power in restraining blessing. I remind myself often to stay only where people receive me. It's a reality of life that healthy people will not stay long where they are not respected. Find where you are welcome, and invest your time there.

ENEMY ALERT

"Simon, Simon, Satan has asked to sift each of you like wheat."
Luke 22:31

A shocking discrepancy appears when pollsters ask how many people believe in God, and then how many people believe in the devil. A significant number of people who believe in God refuse to believe there is an enemy. Here Jesus is telling one of his closest friends that the enemy is asking to break him into little pieces. The sun may be shining and the road may be level and straight for you today, but know that the enemy is looking to sift anyone with great potential. Don't back down, don't turn away, don't be fearful; be wise and courageous. Remember that Jesus in you is far greater than the enemy in this world. Let that put a smile on your face.

MARCH 26

REQUEST

"Then he said, 'Jesus, remember me when you come into your Kingdom.'"
Luke 23:42

There is no confession in this passage, only the request that Jesus remember him. Let your prayer today be that Jesus remembers you, even in the midst of your trial. Certainly He will, just as he remembered this condemned man who hung on a cross beside Him.

COMPLAINTS

"But Jesus replied,
'Stop complaining about what I said.'"
John 6:43

When we pause for introspection, we often notice things about ourselves that others have been aware of for a while. For instance, do you catch yourself when you grumble and complain? Or do you need others to point it out to you? Here, Jesus interrupts His own teaching to tell people to stop complaining. Complaints not only weaken us, they weaken the people we are talking to and the people we are talking about. In fact, I believe the only way we can receive a new idea is when we stop complaining about an old problem. What are you grumbling about today? Can you stop? Will you stop? Jesus has a new teaching for you.

MARCH 28

DRAWN

"For no one can come to me unless the Father who sent me draws them to me."
John 6:44a

It's nice to know God is in the drawing business. He is pursuing us, wooing us, and pulling us toward Him. Don't resist Him. Look for Him, wait for Him, and run to Him. Every time God has ever drawn me it has been for the best. We are not alone. He wants you more than you want Him.

KNOW & DO

"Jesus replied, 'Your mistake is that you don't know the Scriptures, and you don't know the power of God.'"
Matthew 22:29

Here Jesus is correcting some religious leaders on their thinking and teaching. First, He points out they don't know their data, the Scriptures. On top of that, they don't know the power behind the data, the "power of God." This is a double whammy: to first not know the truth and then not realize its power. The writer James tells us to be not just hearers of the word but also doers (James 1:22-25). When you are a doer, you experience the power of the truth you have learned. Don't just read the page; absorb the truth. Don't just absorb the truth; live it. Look for opportunities today to live out the truths you know.

MARCH 30

GREATNESS

"So if you ignore the least commandment and teach others to do the same, you will be called the least in the Kingdom of Heaven. But anyone who obeys God's laws and teaches them will be called great in the Kingdom of Heaven." Matthew 5:19b

To practice and teach is to take steps towards greatness. However, it is far more common in our culture to hear things casually and remember them briefly. Here Jesus is saying that if you don't live out the wisdom and instruction God gives, you will miss a valuable opportunity. But if you live what you believe and translate it into teaching so you are contagious to others, then you are headed for an uncommon life. Today, look for ways to pass on what you learn and live to those around you. I'll do the same. Together, we'll multiply and spread the love, peace, joy, and hope that comes from being followers of the Prince of Peace.

INVESTMENT PORTFOLIO

"Don't store up treasures here on earth, where moths eat them and rust destroys them, and where thieves break in and steal. Store your treasures in heaven…." Matthew 6:19-20a

Personally, I need this reminder all the time. There is a place for things and possessions, isn't there? We ought to not just survive life, but enjoy it. Clearly God created us with senses and an appreciation for beauty. So enjoying beauty and savoring the smell of a flower and the presence of a beautiful home is no sin. But when we invest most of our energy, thoughts, and concerns on things like these that are temporary, we miss the point of being a person who has one foot in eternity. Scripture repeatedly reminds us we are foreigners or strangers on this earth. We are just passing through. Heaven is our real home. Does our checkbook reflect that heaven is our home? Are we giving? Are we tithing? Are we looking for ways to invest our dollars in heaven's economy?

HOPE FOR

APRIL

WHOLEHEARTED

"Jesus replied, 'You must love the Lord your God with all your heart, all your soul, and all your mind.'"
Matthew 22:37

I think it's powerful that the sole verb in this sentence is love. God wants the affection that comes from the heart, soul, and mind. He wants us to love Him with everything we've got. Not just think about Him; that's the process of the mind. Not just be rescued by Him; that's a soul thing. But love Him with the center of our affections—spiritually, emotionally, intellectually. To love from all three areas with everything we have. Not second place, but first place. Our first priority, the preeminent focus of all of our affection.

APRIL 2

CONVICTION

"These people honor me with their lips, but their hearts are far from me."
Matthew 15:8

It's so easy to get in the habit of saying things we don't really mean. The writer of Proverbs reminds us that where there are lots of words, there tends to be sin. That's why it's so important to put a gap between your thoughts, your words, and your actions. Let that gap be a place of meditation, contemplation. When we think about something, we test it and see if it's true. Then we say it, as an affirmation of what we have thoughtfully considered. The power of our words is so significant. The only thing that can mute or dull this power is when we are saying things we don't believe. Today, let us be people who honor God with our hearts, speaking from the deepest part of our hearts about how much He means to us.

VALUES

"...but God knows your hearts. What this world honors is detestable in the sight of God."
Luke 16:15b

Years ago I read a book called *Who Switched the Price Tags* by Tony Campolo. In it he talks about how the values of this world are all turned around, upside down, and inside out in comparison to the values of God's Kingdom. God's Kingdom values people and uses things; our world uses people and values things. Let's be people today who may have and use things, but we love people. Not the other way around.

INTERPRETATION

"He replied, 'You know the saying, 'Red sky at night means fair weather tomorrow; red sky in the morning means foul weather all day.' You know how to interpret the weather signs in the sky, but you don't know how to interpret the signs of the times!" Matthew 16:2-3

This has been one of my favorite passages for some time. Jesus is speaking to people during His time on earth, but His words could just as accurately be said to the current generation. I want to be someone who doesn't just know what is going on in the world. I want to understand and be able to "interpret the signs of the times." To interpret is to have insight about the meaning and significance of information. This requires spiritual knowing. If you are a follower of Jesus, you have the Spirit of God in you. The Holy Spirit gives us insight, not just into what happens around us, but also into why and ultimately, I believe, how to turn these events into a blessing.

DIRECTION

"Direct your children onto the right path, and when they are older, they will not leave it."
Proverbs 22:6

This may be one of the first verses I ever heard, even before my family began attending church. I know my parents claimed this as a significant instruction and promise after they committed their lives to Jesus. This proverb is painful for some people because they feel like they directed their children well, yet their children departed from the path and haven't returned to it. I believe the writer's intent is to communicate a general principle, that when you tend and guide a seed well, you get a good harvest. Jesus tempers this outlook with His reminder that there is an enemy always looking to steal good seed. Meditate on this today and let it encourage you to protect, pray for, and nurture the seed you are sowing into the next generation.

APRIL 6

TRUE KNOWLEDGE

"Fear of the Lord is the foundation of true knowledge, but fools despise wisdom and discipline." Proverbs 1:7

Don't get hung up on the word "fear." This is not the shivering fear of evil; it is the awestruck fear of greatness. Understanding the power of place—not just in the world, but in God's plan—is the beginning of really knowing things. Too often the "smartest people in the room" reject even the notion of God or refuse to consider that there might be something or someone bigger than human beings. This really does lead to foolishness. Perhaps not in a classroom or in a grade book, but ultimately in what Scripture calls the Lamb's Book of Life, the ledger of all who know and love God. Start out this morning by thanking God that He is bigger than you, smarter than you, and can do what you cannot do. This is the beginning of true knowledge.

NOBLE

"A wife of noble character who can find? She is worth far more than rubies."
Proverbs 31:10 (NIV)

This rhetorical question is intended to remind us that like rubies, nobility is rare. It's so easy to be common. By definition, common means to be like the majority or the masses. But to be noble isn't just having affluence; it is being regal. Someone who acts like royalty and thinks like royalty. Let's remind ourselves today that we are children of the King, sons and daughters of the Most High, and the beneficiaries of a wonderful future.

COMPASS

"There is a path before each person that seems right, but it ends in death."
Proverbs 14:12

You cannot judge the "rightness" of a pattern, a lifestyle, or a decision based on temporary appearances. Or based on what the majority thinks, what the newspapers are talking about, or what laws and lawyers say is appropriate. In the end, this can destroy not only a culture but the heart and soul of a people. I have found it is best to make the culture conform to the truths of God's word, instead of asking the word to conform to the culture. So many have run ashore trying to keep up with what this world says leads to life but ultimately ends in death. Find the word, follow the word, celebrate the word, and let the word change you, change your family, and then change our world.

RESTRAINT

"Where there is no revelation, people cast off restraint; but blessed is the one who heeds wisdom's instruction."
Proverbs 29:18 (NIV)

So many people miss the significance of God's principles and commands. They frame them in their mind as a negative force instead of a beautiful blessing. I think we have all seen the wreckage that comes from casting off restraint. Most powerful things need restraint. Fire needs restraint. Energy needs restraint in order for it to be a blessing and not a curse. Let the principles and commandments in God's word be your restraint, not to hold you back, but to drive you forward with power and energy for you to be the greatest possible blessing.

APRIL 10

APPRECIATION

"Every time I think of you,
I give thanks to my God."
Philippians 1:3

Which people do you think of every day? Your children? Your spouse? Your parents? Key people in your business? People from your past who have influenced your life? Or maybe you're preoccupied with thoughts of people you aren't thankful for: enemies or people who have hurt or betrayed you. Spend your energy today giving thanks to God for the people you love most. As my mentor Fulton Buntain used to say, "The things you appreciate tend to get better and the things you depreciate tend to get worse."

HONOR

"Dear brothers and sisters, honor those who are your leaders...."
1 Thessalonians 5:12a

Honor has almost become like oxygen to my life. I am looking for people who live honorable lives and trying to spend time with them. I am examining my life in light of how I can be a more honorable man. I am certainly conscious of those who honor me. If we all spent our energy making more room for honor, we would make the world a sweeter place. Be a man or a woman of honor today and give honor to those who are your leaders.

APRIL 12

SAME

"This is my commandment: Love each other in the same way I have loved you."
John 15:12

Jesus is asking us to mimic Him. All children learn first by mimicking. Before they ever take a class, they watch their mom or dad and do what they do. Jesus is saying to his followers, "Don't just love; love each other. And don't just love each other; do it the way I do it." We see it in the pages of Scripture and we feel it in the Spirit that lives in us: Jesus loves us unconditionally, passionately, without constraint, and with deep concern. That is how I am going to try to love people today.

GREATEST LOVE

"There is no greater love than to lay down one's life for one's friends."
John 15:13

This statement is not talking about dying physically for someone you care about, although Jesus ultimately did so for us and many have done so for others. There's no question physical sacrifice of one's life is a powerful expression of love. But in the city where I live, a more immediate opportunity to "lay down one's life for one's friends" is to lay down our preferences, lay down our opinions, lay down our rights, lay down our pride, and serve people with love. Sounds difficult, doesn't it? Yet there is no greater love. Let's try it today.

APRIL 14

CARGO

"Fearing for their lives, the desperate sailors shouted to their gods for help and threw the cargo overboard to lighten the ship."
Jonah 1:5a

Sailors in ancient times were very superstitious people. Perhaps they still are. These particular sailors were doing what we all do in the midst of a "storm" in our lives: crying out to their gods and throwing things and people overboard. But if your god is false and has no power, perhaps you should do it the other way around and throw your gods and idols overboard. Who do you worship today? Is Jesus really the center of your life? If He is, then cry out to Him and throw the stuff overboard. But if Jesus isn't number one, throw something else overboard.

THROUGH

"He had to go through Samaria on the way."
John 4:4

John makes it seem with his words that Samaria wasn't really the ultimate destination. It was just a town to pass through on the way to somewhere else. Yet Jesus had a notable encounter there. He changed a woman who changed a city. I am sure you have goals and dreams you feel like you haven't yet accomplished. Maybe today feels like one more day to live through on the way to somewhere you have your sights set on reaching. Some of Jesus' best work happens "on the way." Look for Him today. You might meet Him in an unexpected place at an unexpected time.

APRIL 16

SELF-CONTROL

"A person without self-control is like a city with broken-down walls."
Proverbs 25:28

Self-control not only protects us from ourselves, it protects us from others. In this crazy world we live in there are always people looking for a mark or an opportunity to exploit. Your self-control keeps evil people at bay and helps you build confidence. A lack of self-control dilutes your confidence as well as your protection.

PRACTICAL MATTERS

"One day the guild of prophets came to Elisha and said, 'You can see that this place where we're living under your leadership is getting cramped—we have no elbow room.'"
2 Kings 6:1 (MSG)

Radically committed Jesus people, spiritually enlightened men and women of God, and people who walk and talk with their Creator every day, still have practical problems. Spiritual connection is not a guarantee of physical convenience. Progress and power in the supernatural does not equate to being able to ignore the natural. Be a radical Jesus follower today, but keep your feet on the ground with the rest of us, please.

APRIL 18

NUMBERS

"He said, 'Don't worry about it—there are more on our side than on their side.'"
2 Kings 6:16 (MSG)

God's math is different and frankly much better than our math. One of God's is better than a hundred of someone else's. It's even sweeter when God's number is not only better than ours, but bigger. God outnumbers His enemies. When you are doing His work, He is outnumbering your enemies too. You may not see it, but those who are with you are greater than those who are against you. Proceed accordingly.

EMPTY

"For they have given a tiny part of their surplus,
but she, poor as she is,
has given everything she has."
Luke 21:4

Don't be afraid to dip into your reservoir: your emotional reservoir, your free time reservoir, and your financial reservoir. God can fill whatever you empty for Him. When this woman emptied herself out, she also opened herself up to a miracle. Give of the time you don't have, the money you don't have, the energy you don't have and see what Jesus can do.

APRIL 20

ENGAGE

"Keep watch and pray, so that you will not give in to temptation."
Matthew 26:41a

To pray is to engage God in the endeavor. To watch is to engage your intellect. Having God on your side is not permission to turn your brain off. Watch for what you know. Watch for what you suspect. Pay attention and also engage God. He will keep His eyes on things you cannot see, but we have to do our part. Don't get lazy on yourself.

TEACHER

"You call me 'Teacher' and 'Lord,' and you are right, because that's what I am."
John 13:13

Let Jesus teach you. He knows so much. He knows about victory and defeat. He knows about yesterday and today and tomorrow and the future. Let Him be your teacher. If He's just an "enlightened whisper" in your mind, you're missing His power. He is Teacher and Lord. Let Him be the boss, let Him be the Savior. Give Him your best attention today.

LIGHT

"If you follow me, you won't have to walk in darkness, because you will have the light that leads to life."
John 8:12b

The darker it gets, the harder it is to see. The harder it is to see, the more things you bump into. The more things you bump into, the more you get hurt. Let Jesus into the dark places. Less hurt, more happiness, more insight. Jesus, Jesus, Jesus, as much Jesus as you can get. Get Him!

CELEBRATE

"We had to celebrate this happy day. For your brother was dead and has come back to life! He was lost, but now he is found!"
Luke 15:32

Maybe the greatest disease among attitudes is scarcity. When was the last time you were genuinely happy for someone else? Not wishing you had gotten what they had gotten, not wondering what they had done to deserve it, but truly happy something had bloomed in their life? Find someone who is growing and thriving and bless them. They might have come through a tough season. They might be headed toward another one. Celebrate with them. Particularly be happy when people walk away from sin and death into forgiveness and life.

APRIL 24

BELIEF

"There is no judgment against anyone who believes in him."
John 3:18a

There is something about belief that opens the door to possibility and closes the door on judgment. Everyone celebrates John 3:16 but John 3:18 reminds us that it's not just what Jesus did, but it's our believing in what He did and who He is, that rescues us from being condemned. Believe today. Be free today. Whoever believes is not condemned.

ASSIGNMENT

"We must quickly carry out the tasks assigned us by the one who sent us."
John 9:4a

Opportunity is before you today. Don't miss it. Look for it. Don't search for obstacles; they're in plain sight. Look for opportunity and take it. You have breath in your lungs, you have a spring in your step, you have one more day to make a difference. Go do it!

APRIL 26

ALL

"Jesus replied, "'You must love the Lord your God with all....'""
Matthew 22:37a

All is such a significant word. Jesus goes on to say all our heart, all our soul, all our mind. He's pulling everything in, in every category. Use your intellect today and make it submit to Jesus. Use your psychology, use your spirituality, use your passion today. May they all serve the Nazarene and His objectives: love, joy, peace, patience, kindness, goodness, faithfulness, gentleness, and self-control (Galatians 5:22-23a). May these things appear in us when we give our all to Jesus today.

APPETITE

"And don't be concerned about what to eat and what to drink. Don't worry about such things."
Luke 12:29

We are a people of appetites. Our appetites drive us. They set our direction and often control our moods. Yet Jesus casually says, "Don't worry about it. You don't work for your appetites; your appetites work for you." Claim leadership of your life and make your appetites submit today. You are a Jesus man. You are a Jesus woman. He is in the driver's seat.

APRIL 28

BLUEPRINT

"We can make our plans, but the Lord determines our steps."
Proverbs 16:9

Both of these have to happen today. Make your plans and invest in them wholeheartedly. Put your back into it, as my dad likes to say. Also put your prayers into it. Ask Jesus to be part of whatever is ahead. Ask Him to give you wisdom and inspiration.

RENEWAL

"But those who trust in the Lord will find new strength."
Isaiah 40:31a

Every day drains us of our strength. There is no use denying it. We wake up refreshed and go to bed exhausted. Today, focus on the source of your renewal. It's not just sleep, a nice pillow, or a comfortable mattress. It's Jesus. He renews you not just in body, but also in spirit and soul. Thank Him for it today.

APRIL 30

TRUE WORSHIP

"But the time is coming—indeed it's here now—when true worshipers will worship the Father in spirit and in truth."
John 4:23a

Our appearance matters. That's why we get up every day, shower, comb our hair, brush our teeth, and put our best foot forward. Jesus is telling this woman that it's not the outside that matters, but rather the inside, the spirit, where we worship Jesus in the most pure way. By all means, look your best today. But before you do, make sure you are your best today. Talk to Jesus, spirit to Spirit.

MAY

MAY 1

MOUNTAINS

"Then Jesus said to the disciples, 'Have faith in God. I tell you the truth, you can say to this mountain....'"
Mark 11:22-23a

Everybody has faith in something. Where you place it is what matters most. The "positive thinking" world would tell you it's the positive faith itself that matters, but really it's where your faith is placed that is most important. Most definitely, you will face a mountain. Most definitely, faith will move it if your faith is in God. You know His first name: Jesus. Are you facing a mountain today? Talk to Jesus about it.

THIS

"Jesus replied, 'The most important commandment is this:'"
Mark 12:29a

Not every commandment is equal, though they are all impactful. Jesus is telling us to pay attention to the most important commandments. Life is about focus and priorities. Jesus is about to tell us what matters most. When He is about to speak, we should pay attention.

MAY 3

MUST

"And you must love the Lord your God with all your heart, all your soul, all your mind, and all your strength." Mark 12:30

Yesterday, Jesus was about to tell us the most important commandment. Here it is. He directs His listeners back to Himself. He says, "Give Me everything you've got. This is the most important commandment: to give it all to Me." Wow. The audacity of this commandment, the totality that it requires. Can you imagine saying that out loud? To a bunch of people gathered around listening to you? It's something that can only be said by the One who gave them everything they have to give. No wonder Jesus is able to make the brash statement that this is the most important commandment. Let's do this today. Let's live the most important thing. Let's give Jesus our heart, soul, mind, and strength. Give Him your all today.

RETURN

"If the master returns and finds that the servant has done a good job, there will be a reward."
Luke 12:43

Friend, He is coming back! And when He does, we want to be found putting our back into the most important work. In a world full of "selfies" we want to be about sowing seed into others. If He came back today, what would He find you doing or being about? Today, be about His business. Put your back into it.

MAY 5

HEART

"Jesus knew what they were saying...."
Mark 8:17

Oh, wow. Wouldn't it be sobering if we lived like Jesus was aware of what we say out loud? Aware of our whispers and not just our public social media posts? This is why it's so important to be generous of heart and not just of word. When you are generous of heart, you never have to wonder what Jesus is aware of. It is all good. Work on your heart today. Your conversation will flow out of that place.

USE

"'You have eyes—can't you see? You have ears—can't you hear?' Don't you remember anything at all?"
Mark 8:18

Jesus is reminding us it's not good enough to just have the "right equipment." We have to use it in the right way. Elsewhere Scripture tells us to focus on the good, to think on things that are pure and full of life (Philippians 4:8). Do you have ears to hear the best or the worst? Do you have eyes to see fault, or eyes to see the fingerprints of Jesus all over the lives of people around you and your life, too? Today, let's listen for the voice and look for the fingerprints of Jesus.

MAY 7

ECONOMY

"What this world honors is detestable in the sight of God."
Luke 16:15b

It never hurts to remind yourself that up is down and down is up, that in is out. We live in an inside out world. The "price tags" have been switched. What is valuable to God has been deemed worthless by our modern culture. What is priceless to this world is mud-pies to our Creator. Don't splash around in the mud. God has priceless lives for us. Let's live them.

SINCE

"And since I, your Lord and Teacher, have washed your feet, you ought to wash each other's feet."
John 13:14

Jesus didn't ask us to do much, but He did ask us to wash one another's feet. I believe He meant this literally, and we can also expand the principle to other ways of serving each other. There is something special about a father washing the feet of his children, a business man washing the feet of his employees, and a pastor washing the feet of his congregation. The Bible says very little about leadership but a whole lot about followership. Be a good follower today. Wash the feet of someone. It blesses both of you.

WATCHED

"I have given you an example to follow. Do as I have done to you."
John 13:15

Jesus knew His behavior was being watched. Do you know yours is, too? Are you aware you are setting an example? Live like people are watching and as if you want the world to be better. I will try to do the same today.

BROKEN

"God blesses those who are poor and realize their need for him, for the Kingdom of Heaven is theirs."
Matthew 5:3

No one likes being poor in spirit, broken. But it's nice to know there is a hidden treasure. The treasure is the character that comes from it. Something about brokenness leads to the Kingdom. Follow the map of brokenness to the hidden treasure of the Kingdom.

NEED

"God blesses those who mourn,
for they will be comforted."
Matthew 5:4

The Bible surprises us when it talks about the benefits of being needy. Our culture, like many others, prefers facades of strength to the reality of brokenness. But only the needy receive. Only the mourning receive comfort. Only the hungry receive food, and only sick receive medicine. Admit your need today and ask Jesus to meet it.

HUMBLE

"God blesses those who are humble,
for they will inherit the whole earth."
Matthew 5:5

If ever there was a countercultural notion, this is it. The meek and humble generally don't inherit much, but the strong grab, scrape, scrap, and claw for their inheritance. Here we read there is something about the quiet, the prayerful, the humble that makes Jesus remember them. An inheritance is something that is left for you by someone else. I believe God has left something behind for people who embrace humility. You may have a great inheritance stored up for you. Live today as if you are going to inherit something great.

MAY 13

HUNGER

"God blesses those who hunger and thirst for justice, for they will be satisfied."
Matthew 5:6

You have to build up an appetite for good things. Most of us, once we have tasted junk food, crave it more readily than the things that nurture us. I think it's the same with our spirits. Build up an appetite for righteousness. Knock off the spiritual junk food and acquire a taste for something that is good for your soul. You will crave it and find yourself filled to the brim with joy.

MERCY

"God blesses those who are merciful,
for they will be shown mercy."
Matthew 5:7

I don't believe in karma and I don't believe in fate. I do believe that when you sow one type of seed it tends to grow into a harvest. When you plant mercy, you tend to have a harvest of it later. Don't follow your impulses. Follow your principles. Be merciful today to people. You most certainly will need it in return someday.

MAY 15

PURE

"God blesses those whose hearts are pure,
for they will see God."
Matthew 5:8

It's not as if God will appear to these people and not to the rest of us. It's just that the pure of heart are not so cynical that they miss Him. I believe God wants to show Himself to us but often we are too selfish, cynical, jaded, and full of doubt to see Him. The pure of heart are looking for the miracle or watching for the hand of Jesus. Put aside other things today and peel the scales off of your eyes. God will be working around you. Perhaps you can catch a glimpse of Him.

PEACE

"God blesses those who work for peace, for they will be called the children of God."
Matthew 5:9

I don't know if Jesus meant to end His talk with peacemakers, but if He did, maybe it's because there are so few of them. When you have found a peacemaker, you have found something rare. Not the peacekeepers who cover up stuff, but the ones who see the worst and make the most of it. They will be identified as the children of God. I like that. I want to be associated with Jesus' family. I am going to make the most of the conflicts that surround me so I might be a peacemaker today. Let's do it together.

MAY 17

REVOLUTIONARY

"Take my yoke upon you. Let me teach you, because I am humble and gentle at heart, and you will find rest for your souls."
Matthew 11:29

Find another candidate, prime minister, president, king, or potentate that openly says, "I am gentle and humble." I think you'll be looking for a long time to find a person like that. Leaders generally want to remind us of their strength. Jesus was a revolutionary leader who said, "I am gentle. I won't hurt anybody. I am humble to the core." Then He challenged us to find rest in His gentleness and humility, not in the strength and braggadocio of our culture. What a contrast He is.

CHILDLIKE

"Then he said, 'I tell you the truth, unless you turn from your sins and become like little children, you will never get into the Kingdom of Heaven.'"
Matthew 18:3

Children are comfortable with dependence, looking for fun, and trusting for provision. Let's do this today. Think like a child.

MAY 19

DIFFERENT

"But among you it will be different."
Matthew 20:26a

Jesus is drawing a contrast between the leaders and authorities of the world, and those who follow Him. Remember this today. In the midst of the way this world operates, following Jesus "will be different." We follow a different drum beat and we dance a different dance because of it. It's okay to be different. In fact, it's not only okay, it is a necessity.

LEADING

"Whoever wants to be a leader among you must be your servant."
Matthew 20:26b

I read this sentence over and over just to make sure it hasn't changed. Could Jesus really be serious that greatness comes through serving? Could He really? I guess we will never know until we try.

MAY 21

EXAMPLE

"So practice and obey whatever they tell you, but don't follow their example."
Matthew 23:3a

Jesus is saying that to live in this world we have to honor the authorities God has put in place, but we do not have to mimic them. In fact, we can't. Honor the authority above you, but look to Jesus for how to live your life. Following Jesus' example makes us more like Jesus. Following the world's example makes us more bankrupt like the world.

CHOSEN

"You didn't choose me. I chose you."
John 15:16a

We spend our whole lives wanting to be chosen for the right teams, for the right roles, by the right people. Here the Creator of the universe says, "I pick you, I see you, I choose you, I select you, I love you, I want you, I crave you. Even though you were never interested in me." Jesus sees past our indifference toward Him and He indulges His passion towards us. Doesn't that make you smile?

MAY 23

CONSEQUENCE

"So every tree that does not produce good fruit is chopped down and thrown into the fire."
Matthew 7:19

It's sobering to be reminded that our life is consequential. From one angle, judgment is menacing and consequences can induce fear. But a meaningful life will always have consequence. The point is to live a life that produces good fruit. Don't live a life of regret. Live a life of rejoicing. It's been said the pain of discipline is less than the pain of regret. Let's live today with this in mind.

MANY TOWNS

"...a large crowd that had gathered from many towns to hear him."
Luke 8:4b

Don't be fooled by the headlines of prominent papers and magazines. People are coming to Jesus from every town on earth. Totalitarian states cannot stop them. Borders and fences and walls cannot prevent them. Language differences barely hinder them at all. People are coming to Jesus from your town, my town, that town, the next town. Isn't it wonderful to look around and know that everywhere you see is Jesus' territory?

MAY 25

ADVOCATE

"But when the Father sends the Advocate as my representative—that is, the Holy Spirit—he will teach you everything and will remind you of everything I have told you."
John 14:26

You can earn a master's degree and still be ignorant. You can forget much of what you once knew. But it's nice to know the Holy Spirit will always be available to teach you. He lives in you every day, sunny days and cloudy days, holidays and work days. He is willing to teach you not just about broad topics but about how He can help you, how He can change you, how He can encourage you. Then He reminds you of His principles so you are never without a resource you can tap into for wisdom.

WHO & WHERE

"But from now on the Son of Man will be seated in the place of power at God's right hand."
Luke 22:69

Jesus was not just a teacher. He was not just a prophet. He was not an enlightened guru. He was God in the flesh, and He has returned to the place He occupied before He came to earth. Scripture says it clearly to make sure we understand it. Jesus of Nazareth was God in the flesh. Serve Him, worship Him, and work for Him today.

MAY 27

CAMPAIGN

"But Jesus replied, 'We must go on to other towns as well, and I will preach to them, too. That is why I came.'"
Mark 1:38

This verse hangs on a wall in the offices where I work. I love it. It reminds me that Jesus moved from town to town because He didn't want anyone forgotten. He is in your town now and He is still on the move. Like all great campaigns, like all great marches, He is building momentum and winning hearts and minds. Be a part of the greatest campaign in history.

FORGIVENESS

"...the Son of Man has the authority on earth to forgive sins."
Mark 2:10a

This is good news! Don't go another second with unforgiven sin. Talk to Jesus right now about your worst moments and ask for His forgiveness. They will be completely wiped out, impotent of any power to hurt you for eternity.

MAY 29

PRAYER

"He went on a little farther and bowed with his face to the ground, praying...."
Matthew 26:39a

This is Jesus praying. This is Jesus, face to the ground, crying out to His Father. If Jesus prayed this way, shouldn't you, shouldn't I, shouldn't we? Let's pray for our country, our city, our church, our pastor, our family. Let's be like Jesus and talk to the Father today.

LIGHT

"Jesus spoke to the people once more and said, 'I am the light of the world.'"
John 8:12a

Don't you love the sunrise in the morning after hours of darkness? The beauty of the world can be seen again. The light brings the flowers out, cues the birds to sing, and it wakes us up, too. Wake up today; the light is shining. A day without Jesus is a dark day. Let your light shine to everyone you work with today. Be bold about it.

MAY 31

SERVE

"For even the Son of Man came not to be served but to serve..."
Mark 10:45a

Jesus came with an agenda, with a strategic plan. It was simple, replicable, and everyone can copy it. He came to serve the poor and the rich, the illiterate and the well-educated. Serving changes things. He didn't come to sit on a throne. He came to die on a cross, the ultimate form of service. Look for someone to serve today. Let's copy Jesus. Let's be servants for 12 hours and see what happens.

JUNE

JUNE 1

SIGNIFICANCE

"so it is with Christ's body. We are many parts of one body...."
Romans 12:5a

As I get older, I'm noticing more aches and pains as I get moving each morning. How about you? One side benefit of these groanings is that I'm becoming more conscious of all the little parts that make up all that is Dean. You may be feeling insignificant this morning. You are not insignificant. When you hurt, we all hurt. When you win, we all win. Forgive me if I have not reminded you lately how precious you are to me, to others, to the One who made you. The body of Jesus is better because of you.

BELONGING

"...and we all belong to each other."
Romans 5:12b

Belonging feels so good. In fact, is there a worse feeling than the feeling of not belonging or being out of place? I am sure there are tragedies larger than that, but it does ache when we don't have a conscious sense of belonging to somebody. I belong to you. You belong to me. What connects us is not agreement on politics or shared experience, but that we have Jesus in common. He is the great connector. We belong to each other. We belong together.

JUNE 3

UNITY

"How wonderful it is, how pleasant, for God's people to live together in harmony."
Psalm 133:1 (GNT)

I suppose it's a sad commentary that it's really "wonderful" in part because it is so rare. If unity were commonplace, I don't think we would rejoice over it as much. Have you done something lately to build unity between Jesus people? We don't have to put any thought into dividing; we do it naturally. We segregate around taste, music preference, teaching style, schedule, dress code, secondary doctrinal differences, and anything else we choose to give importance to. But to unite, we have to work harder. Think of somebody you can unite with today just because they love Jesus.

PEACE

"...you were chosen to live together in peace."
Colossians 3:15b (CEV)

Never get so comfortable with tension and disagreement that you start to believe it's your fate. Dis-ease is not your destiny. You were chosen, selected, and set aside to live together in peace. Jesus is the great peacemaker. Wherever there is not peace in your life, try to insert a little more Jesus.

SHARING

"Share each other's burdens,
and in this way obey the law of Christ."
Galatians 6:2

When we share, we typically share something we have too much of. If we have cake we cannot eat all of, or if we have an abundance of resources, we share. But this instruction is not telling us to share the good stuff we have more than enough of; it says to go ahead and share problems. Divide them up among us. Help each other carry them. This isn't something we do lightly, and it's not something we always do with joy, but it is something we should do regularly.

COMPREHENSION

"Then Jesus asked them, 'Didn't you ever read this in the Scriptures?'"
Matthew 21:42a

Jesus is about to mention a specific Scripture to His religious critics. But first, He asks what seems like a sarcastic question. As religious leaders, they have memorized the Scriptures; so certainly they have read the one Jesus is about to cite. I believe what He is getting at is not just their intake of the words, but their comprehension of what is really happening in front of them. Today, don't just take in the principles of Jesus as data; take them in as life-changing truths and share them with someone who needs a changed life.

JUNE 7

CORNERSTONE

"The stone that the builders rejected has now become the cornerstone. This is the Lord's doing, and it is wonderful to see."
Matthew 21:42b

Jesus is referring to Himself. He is saying, I may just be one person, but I am the central person. Jesus' centrality in history is not questioned much, but His centrality in our personal lives is often in flux. Don't let Jesus be just another teacher among teachers for you. Let Him be the cornerstone: the person on whom you build your habits, the principles on which you build your moral code, and the truth on which you build your eternity.

SUBMISSION

"My Father! If it is possible, let this cup of suffering be taken away from me. Yet I want your will to be done, not mine."
Matthew 26:39b

Most of us spend a great deal of energy trying to get our way. From our earliest childhood memories, we can recall telling people (or at least thinking the thought), "You're not the boss of me." Here, Jesus is not trying to be the boss; He is submitting to His Father's will. Jesus' assignment is so much bigger and more difficult than mine. Yet I sometimes struggle to accept His assignment and His orders. Today, let's all try to take a more humble, submissive posture and say as Jesus did, "I want Your will to be done, not mine."

JUNE 9

DISARM

"...Jesus told him. 'Those who use the sword will die by the sword.'"
Matthew 26:52b

Oh my! What a troublesome thought that you and I are shish-kebabbed by our own silliness, stupidity, and mistakes. As followers of Jesus, we don't have to be people of the sword. We can be people of peace. No matter what situation you are in, try to keep your sword in its scabbard. Instead of drawing out a weapon, pull out a blessing and bless those who curse you. You may be the only one in the room who does.

HIS NAME

"...so that the Father will give you whatever you ask for, using my name."
John 15:16b

I find it curious that Jesus literally tells us to use His name and yet so many religious people rarely speak it. We talk about "church," "Christianity," "ministry," "fellowship." But Jesus doesn't give a reward for talking about church, ministry, or ourselves. There is promise and power in the name of Jesus. Any time, any place, in any language you mention Jesus, people are fascinated. Try to work His name into conversations today. Not in a religious way, but in a warm, personal way, and see what happens.

JUNE 11

WORLDVIEW

"God loved the world..."
John 3:16a (NCV)

Seven billion people occupy this globe right now and Jesus was unequivocal in stating how His Father felt about them all. Whatever their nationality, language, race, ethnicity, religion, size, shape, age, or personality, God loves them. Jesus loves them. "The world" was Jesus' big "why." They are the reason He came. Are there people you struggle to love? Let God show His love for them through you today.

SO MUCH

"...so much that he gave his one and only Son so that whoever believes in him may not be lost, but have eternal life."
John 3:16b

It has almost become common at major football games, basketball games, or other types of events, to see someone holding up a sign with John 3:16 on it. But I never tire of reminding myself that God gave His all and Jesus gave His all, so everyone could have an opportunity for eternal life. Sadly, many reject it. Many ignore it. And some dip their toe in it but never dive in. Today, I am going to be an "all in" follower of Jesus and try to enjoy all the best He has for me.

JUNE 13

RELATIONSHIP

"Not everyone who calls out to me, 'Lord! Lord!' will enter the Kingdom of Heaven."
Matthew 7:21a

Meditate on this today: a title or label of "Christian," or even a leadership title like "Pastor," isn't enough. You can't claim relationship with Jesus by just putting on a nametag. You have to live in relationship. This should not be a cause for fear. This should be a cause for introspection. Every day we fail. Every day we get up and aim to do better. But through it all, is Jesus with you? He wants to be. Do you let Him in? Don't be a follower in name only. Be an emissary who takes orders and does so with a smile. Be a happy ambassador today.

AGREEMENT

"I also tell you this: If two of you agree here on earth concerning anything you ask, my Father in heaven will do it for you."
Matthew 18:19

Jesus is giving us something to truly ponder: that our prayers, offered in unity, even with just one other person, release things in heaven. Most of us know that heaven has impact on earth, that the supernatural steers the natural. Have you thought about how significant your prayers are in giving heaven direction? Today, connect with another Jesus person and commit to spend two minutes of your day praying in Jesus' name for the same request. Let's see what happens.

JUNE 15

AMONG

"For where two or three gather together as my followers, I am there among them."
Matthew 18:20

We are always meeting with people, aren't we? My goodness, I am always bouncing from one meeting to another. This statement is not just a prompt to gather. It is a prompt to gather with Jesus as the convener. Is Jesus a part of your circle? Does He come up in your pow-wows? Is He mentioned in your soirées? Is He invited to the dinner table? Let's include Him in even the smallest gatherings we have. I know you will see a difference for the positive.

CAUTION

"Jesus told them,
'Don't let anyone mislead you.'"
Matthew 24:4

Don't turn your brain off. Not everyone who says they are doing things "in love" is really doing so. Sometimes they deceive even themselves. You have to be the guard of your mind. Your life takes the direction of the people you believe. Who do you trust? Whose report do you believe? I am a better man today because I believed the right people when they gave me counsel. Frankly, I am also a better man because I was watching out for lies and liars. The world is full of both. Be careful who you believe.

JUNE 17

OPEN DOOR

"I know all the things you do, and I have opened a door for you that no one can close."
Revelation 3:8a

Do you live like you have an open door in front of you? Or do you fear God is plotting against you? People conspire and the enemy opposes, but God says, "I know exactly what you have done and I still place an open door before you." Walk with confidence today. The writer of Proverbs reminds us that while the wicked flee even when no one is pursuing them, the righteous are as bold as a lion (Proverbs 28:1). Be as bold as a lion today.

TENACITY

"You have little strength, yet you obeyed my word and did not deny me."
Revelation 3:8b

The book of Revelation is about the end times. So one has to ponder how wonderful it will be to get to the end and have Jesus say, "I know you are worn out, but you did it." Keep going today. Don't let a weary spirit keep you from being an active body. Don't let a discouraged mind keep you from having an encouraging mouth. Speak life. Do good while you have time.

ON BEHALF

"And anyone who welcomes a little child like this on my behalf is welcoming me."
Matthew 18:5

Wherever you go in the world, wherever trouble and mayhem are stirring up people, you will find followers of Jesus reaching out to children. This is neither accident nor coincidence. We are not "do-gooders." We are following a principle Jesus laid out for us with His very own words. I have seen it time and time again, in war torn countries, in environments where people live under totalitarian rule, and when meeting with earthquake victims. The hands of Jesus are being extended to little people. Do you have young people in your life in whom you are investing? Make room and make time for the little ones. Jesus takes it personally, in the best possible way.

WHEN

"Direct your children onto the right path, and when they are older, they will not leave it."
Proverbs 22:6

This verse has troubled many parents. Surely children grow up to have wills of their own. Sometimes they choose poorly. This proverb is a general affirmation that all of the good investments you have made in your children are not wasted, even if you have not yet seen the fruit. Notice the word "older." It might take a while, mom or dad, but hang in there. The truth you put in your children is powerful. Trust in it.

JUNE 21

BEGINNING

"The fear of the Lord is the beginning of knowledge, but fools despise wisdom and instruction."
Proverbs 1:7 (NIV)

My father taught me to drive. When he did, he started by explaining the power and responsibility of being "behind the wheel." He explained all the places a car could take me and all of the danger that is posed. When you are walking with the Almighty God, there is a lot of power and a lot of responsibility. Used correctly, it will take you to the heights. We have to be careful to have more of Jesus and less of ourselves, because religion hurts. Pain and deception is the beginning of disaster, but a fear of the Lord is the beginning of real knowledge and wisdom.

WORTH

"A wife of noble character who can find?
She is worth far more than rubies."
Proverbs 31:10 (NIV)

Rubies are made in the earth and discovered. They are pulled out of their environment and polished for the appreciation of all who see them. It is rare to find a ruby, and the more valuable it is, the more expensive it is. The writer of Proverbs is saying that if we go to that much work to acquire an inanimate object and value it so highly, how much more effort should we invest in finding and appreciating value in people, particularly a partner like a spouse? Today, look for the best in the people nearest to you. Look at the people you work with, the people you live near, and of course the people you live with. See how rare they really are and what a gift they have been to you. Tell them.

JUNE 23

FLAWLESS

"Every word of God is flawless."
Proverbs 30:5a (NIV)

Not every word God gives you is easy. Not every word is an affirmation of something you have done. Sometimes the words are challenging, and sometimes the words remind us we have a long way to go. Yet every word is flawless. Who are you going to trust? Are you going to trust your emotions? Are you going to trust your instincts? Both of those can fail you in a hurry. Trust God's word, even when you don't understand it. You will see over time it will not fail you. God's words are not a microwave; they are a crockpot. Let them work on you, soften you, season you, and prepare you.

SEE

"Jesus asked, 'Will you never believe in me unless you see miraculous signs and wonders?'"
John 4:48

This morning I want to put the emphasis on "see." Jesus does not say, "unless miracles start happening," because miracles were already happening. He does not say, "unless your friends see it," because clearly they were hearing rumors and stories about all the wonderful things that happen wherever Jesus is. Jesus is saying, apparently with a little lament, that some people just cannot "see" the significance, the deeper truth of what is going on, even if they see the evidence of it with their own eyes. Don't be someone who misses the miracle. Don't be somebody who cannot see it, even though everybody else is seeing it. Jesus is still working and still doing miracles. Are you looking? Are you seeing? Or are your eyes closed?

JUNE 25

LEFT

"Then Jesus left them and went away."
Matthew 16:4b

This brief statement follows a speech Jesus gave—a speech in which He told people they didn't "get it." And after telling them this truth, He left their presence. I sometimes wonder how many people realize Jesus has "left the room." There are so many homes where He is not welcome, so many businesses where He is mocked, and so many churches where He is obscured by religious rules and superficial piety. Jesus has spoken, dropped the mic, and left the room. Today let's invite Him back in. Invite Him one more time to your home, your work place, your gatherings, and see what more you can learn from Jesus.

BREAD OF LIFE

"You have so little faith! Why are you arguing with each other about having no bread?"
Matthew 16:8b

Jesus is willing to feed the hungry. He proved it with five loaves and a couple of fish, even though that was not His primary mission. The crowd was always trying to get Jesus focused on things that were temporal because that's what they were interested in. As Jesus people, let's meet the needs of the hungry belly, but always be attentive to meeting the needs of the hungry heart. Bellies are easier to fill than hearts, and hearts are Jesus' main focus. It's not about the bread; it's about Jesus, who is "the bread of life" (John 6:35).

ONE JOB

"Jesus told them, 'This is the only work God wants from you: Believe in the one he has sent.'"
John 6:29

My friend Doug taught me years ago that this verse is central. So many Jesus people are running around doing things in God's name, yet they are really not sure what the most important thing is. Jesus answered this clearly and succinctly. Your one job is to believe, to believe Jesus is who He said He is, to believe He is working in your life. Practice your belief today. Trust Him with something that is seemingly impossible and see what He does. This is your one job.

BEACON

"'It was not because of his sins or his parents' sins,' Jesus answered. 'This happened so the power of God could be seen in him.'"
John 9:3

God is not being cruel here. Jesus is not saying God gives people problems so they can be a billboard for His miracles. He is disputing an ancient theology that still exists today: that somehow "karma" or "payback" is God's system. God's system is not payback, but grace. Jesus is simply pointing out that God allows the good and the bad, and redeems all of it so that it can call His children home. When I was a child, my mother would ring a bell when it was dinnertime to remind us in case we had forgotten about her and the meal that was being prepared. The pain of this world and Jesus' intervention in it, is like a dinner bell calling us home.

JUNE 29

EYE PROTECTION

"And if your eye causes you to sin, gouge it out and throw it away. It's better to enter eternal life with only one eye than to have two eyes and be thrown into the fire of hell."
Matthew 18:9

Thankfully, Jesus is not asking people to literally poke their eyes out. We know this because His disciples were not blind. If He had intended this command literally, our society would be a land of blind people. Immodesty, violence, indulgence, and hurtful and vicious words are all in plain sight every day—published, broadcast, and displayed by the culture around us. This week I am going to be thoughtful about what I lay my eyes on. For some, it's time to lay down the "mature content." For many of us, it's time to lay down the newspaper or social media.

LIKE

"The Pharisee stood by himself and prayed this prayer: 'I thank you, God, that I am not like other people—cheaters, sinners, adulterers. I'm certainly not like that tax collector!'"
Luke 18:11

Normally in our morning devotions, I try to quote Jesus as often as possible. However, today I thought I would quote someone more like us: someone with enough education to be dangerous, someone with enough piety to be self-righteous, someone who knows enough about the rules to start assessing other people. Our prayer this morning should be: "Jesus, help me be more like You." Let's let the Holy Spirit worry about changing others. Comparison deceives and makes prideful, while relationship with Jesus purifies and encourages.

HOPE FOR JULY

APPEAL

"But the tax collector stood at a distance and dared not even lift his eyes to heaven as he prayed. Instead, he beat his chest in sorrow, saying, 'O God, be merciful to me, for I am a sinner.'"
Luke 18:13

Now we see the prayer and remorse of a man who has blown it. The Pharisee we read about yesterday is not satisfied, and the onlooker is mystified, but Jesus is pacified and filled with mercy. This morning, consider saying the prayer, "Help me," or maybe the prayer, "Forgive me." Both of these send Jesus to the rescue and make the enemy flee.

JULY 2

HIS

"My sheep listen to my voice; I know them, and they follow me."
John 10:27

Jesus gives this description of people who are "His." They recognize His voice. This has to do with the ability of our ears—even our inner ear—to hear what His spirit is whispering. They follow. They are people of action. They don't just hear the voice and remain motionless. They go where the voice tells them to go; they do what the voice tells them to do. He knows them personally and intimately. To know is not just to be acquainted or to have just met someone, but to have insight into them and them into you. Isn't that cool that Jesus knows us and we are His?

OBEY

"If you love me, obey my commandments."
John 14:15

Yikes! I wish Jesus hadn't said this. I wish He would say, "If you love Me, then just knock off the bad behavior." Or, "If you love Me, say nice things about Me." But He asks for complete love manifested in trust. Trusting Him enough to do what He asks without protest, without delay. I often do what He asks, but I usually complain first. Even when I do what He asks, I drag my feet. Today, I am going to try to be obedient instantly and with a smile on my face. Will you try it with me?

JULY 4

REVEAL

"...and reveal myself to each of them."
John 14:21b

I love that when Jesus is talking about how much He loves us, He reminds us that He won't just love us from afar; He will show Himself to us. When I visit my children, I often leave little notes for them. When I'm not with them, I send them texts to let them know I'm always thinking about them. I have no doubt Jesus is a far better father than I could ever be. He loves to show Himself to us. He shows us His mercy, His instruction, and His encouragement. Don't be worried. Abba-Father loves you. Look for how He is revealing His love to you today.

CONDUIT

"Do not judge others, and you will not be judged. Do not condemn others, or it will all come back against you. Forgive others, and you will be forgiven."
Luke 6:37

Life has a flow to it. When we live with a critical eye, critical eyes seem to be examining us. When we are using negative words, we tend to be planting seeds of negativity that will bloom in other areas of our life. Jesus reminds us that when we open ourselves to forgiveness, forgiveness flows first to us, and then through us to others. You will be a conduit for something today. Why not let it be forgiveness and grace instead of judgment and condemnation?

JULY 6

IN FULL

"Give, and you will receive. Your gift will return to you in full—pressed down, shaken together to make room for more, running over, and poured into your lap. The amount you give will determine the amount you get back."

Luke 6:38

This verse has been used many times to encourage generosity. To me, it feels more like a general principle. When we give with passion to something, it sows seeds and will reap a harvest that reflects that passion. It is important to remember to not just do the right thing, but also do it with the right heart. I believe life builds momentum. Our passion for sin builds momentum for destruction. Our passion for God's Kingdom builds momentum for eternity. Let's direct our energy toward something wonderful today.

REWARD

"'Yes,' Jesus replied, 'and I assure you that everyone who has given up house or wife or brothers or parents or children, for the sake of the Kingdom of God, will be repaid many times over in this life, and will have eternal life in the world to come.'" Luke 18:29-30

My mentor Fulton Buntain had several sayings he often repeated as reminders. One of these was the statement, "God keeps good books." It was his way of saying that while the small investments we make for Jesus, or the large sacrifices we make to follow His principles, may go unnoticed by others and may not have an immediate return, they are seen by the only "accountant" who matters. Don't worry today. Every good deed you have done is recorded and noted. More importantly, walk in relationship with Jesus for He is the real reward. He is not just a jewel in a crown; He is our real prize.

CAUSE

"But if you cause one of these little ones who trusts in me to fall into sin...."
Matthew 18:6a

Notice that it doesn't say "intend." It says "cause" one of these little ones. Very few people, if we give them the benefit of the doubt, literally intend to lead little ones in the wrong direction. But many of us cause them to go in the wrong direction. Children are subject to the collateral damage of our world in many ways. Today, let's do two things: One, apologize to the little ones in our world, even if they're big now, who might have been caused to go the wrong way because of us. And two, make an investment in today's generation of little ones that will cause them to do something great.

PRIORITIES

"For you are careful to tithe even the tiniest income from your herb gardens, but you ignore the more important aspects of the law—justice, mercy, and faith."
Matthew 23:23b

If we have any sense of spirituality or conscientiousness, we can often find ourselves measuring our goodness by our hours volunteered or our dollars given or rules that we satisfied. Jesus is saying we can nail the letter of the law without capturing the spirit of the law. May these three things be present in our lives today: justice, mercy, and faith. For just this one day, set your tally aside and think on the Spirit.

JULY 10

PLANS

"'For I know the plans I have for you,' says the Lord."
Jeremiah 29:11a

God is not making this up as He goes along. Sometimes we don't understand the plan, but that doesn't mean there isn't one. Consider an empty piece of land with no high rise in sight. But then someone starts digging a hole, and then they start pouring cement, placing rebar, framing, and then, and then, and then. God knows the plan and He is carrying it out today, one step at a time. Relax.

FORESIGHT

"...plans to prosper you and not to harm you, plans to give you hope and a future."
Jeremiah 29:11b (NIV)

God's plan is to prosper (increase) and not to harm (decrease). His plan is to give us a hope and a future. A hope is something in us, and future is a place we are going to be living. So God's plan is to give you something inside you that makes today meaningful and tomorrow possible. Be encouraged. Whatever you are facing is not bigger than God's plan for you. Pass along a little encouragement today to someone else.

JULY 12

DOABLE

"For I can do everything through Christ, who gives me strength."
Philippians 4:13

I am encouraged that there is a strength that goes beyond our muscles. Strength of character, strength of will, strength of knowing there is a plan and purpose to our life. The writer of this letter reminds us that when we operate through Jesus, He gives us strength to go on even when going on seems impossible. Today, face your challenges bravely and your circumstances resolutely, knowing you can do everything God has given you to do through Jesus. Doing things on our own: not so easy. But with Jesus: doable.

CREATION

"In the beginning God created…."
Genesis 1:1a

It's nice to remind ourselves from time to time that God is not a creation of desperate people needing a crutch. Rather, we are the creation of a loving God. From the very beginning, He has been creating. He speaks, and worlds are created. As we speak today, let's be His partners in creating a better world. Speak life, speak hope, and be a blessing to someone.

ABSOLUTE

"Trust in the Lord with all your heart...."
Proverbs 3:5a

The heart is the center of our affections. So trust in Him with all of your passion, with all of your desire, and with the part of you that makes things a priority. Trust in Jesus. Make Him number one. This is the first step to being wise.

DEPEND

"...do not depend on your own understanding."
Proverbs 3:5b

In contrast to trusting Him, trusting ourselves is a fatal mistake. When we trust ourselves, we don't understand our basic make-up. Our frame is not built to carry the weight of the world. Our frame is built to walk in faith and let God carry the weight. Don't lean on or depend on your own understanding. It will break down.

JULY 16

ACKNOWLEDGE

"In all your ways acknowledge Him,
And He will make your paths straight."
Proverbs 3:6 (NASB)

Life's paths are not straight. They are up and down, left and right. Often, you cannot see what is next. But when we acknowledge Him in our all ways, in everything we do, He has a way of making the crooked paths straight and making the hilly path flat. Little by little, through Him we begin to see the order and plan of life. Trust Him today. Let Him straighten out your circumstances.

DISCIPLES

"Therefore, go and make disciples of all the nations...."
Matthew 28:19a

Everybody ought to find somebody to invest in, to find a "disciple," a man or a woman, boy or girl that you are leading. Don't disqualify yourself; you have something to give. Find someone who needs what you have and invest freely.

JULY 18

DEDICATION

"...baptizing them in the name of the Father and the Son and the Holy Spirit."
Matthew 28:19b

Baptism is a dedication. It's a physical something we do that represents a spiritual something we have already done. Jesus is saying, don't just make disciples; dedicate them in the name of God the Father, Jesus the Son, and His Holy Spirit. You are not just investing to invest; you are asking people to be followers of Jesus. It is the best way to live. Frankly, it is the only way to really live.

FUTURE

"For evil people have no future...."
Proverbs 24:20a

Implied here is the opposite: the righteous person has a future. There is something about plotting and executing evil that dries up potential and opportunity. There is something about meditating and acting on righteousness, greatness, and our best impulses that opens doors and draws opportunity. Be someone today who uses your mind and all of your other faculties to give yourself and the people you encounter a better future.

HOPE

"'For I know the plans I have for you,' says the Lord. 'They are plans for good and not for disaster, to give you a future and a hope.'"
Jeremiah 29:11

Is there a verse more often quoted by people who have walked with Jesus for a while? Clearly, its popularity is due to its message: that God's plan is good and His scheming on your behalf is for the positive. Sometimes it appears God has forgotten us or, even worse, His plan seems to be bringing harm. Hold on and hold up hope. He is plotting your victory.

STARTER

"This letter is from Paul, a slave of God and an apostle of Jesus Christ."
Titus 1:1a

Today, let's not look to be leaders; let's look to be servants. We don't serve a boss or a company. We serve our Creator and we are apostles. An apostle is an entrepreneur, a starter of things. So today, I am going to serve God and do whatever He asks me to do. I'm going to be a starter of good things for Jesus, in His name, for His purposes. It is liberating to know I am under orders from the Father and starting projects for Jesus. Let's start good things today.

JULY 22

CONFIDENCE

"This truth gives them confidence that they have eternal life, which God—who does not lie—promised them before the world began."
Titus 1:2

I love that this verse affirms that God never lies. Everyone else does. Even the most honest saints have had moments where they have withheld information they should have shared, or shared information from the wrong vantage point. God is not like that. His purity is absolute and without question. He never lies and He promised things before ages began. Count on His promises. Live with confidence in Him and see the good things that come to pass.

BIG PICTURE

"And if our hope in Christ is only for this life, we are more to be pitied than anyone in the world."
1 Corinthians 15:19

Paul is reflecting to brand new followers of Jesus that there is no hope in the ritual of church, there is no hope in the ritual of daily devotions, and there is no hope in perfect attendance. There is only hope in Jesus, His resurrection, and eternal life with Him. Paul is saying that if we are doing even the best things in this life without a real relationship with Jesus and understanding of who He is, we are to be pitied, not admired. I feel sorry for people who do "good" without having Jesus at the heart of it. I think Paul was onto something. Keep Jesus in it or get out of it entirely.

JULY 24

UNDETERRED

"That is why we never give up."
2 Corinthians 4:16a

So important! Nothing bad even has to happen for us to lose heart. Just the aging process and the drain of energy from everyday living can cause us to lose our enthusiasm. Paul is telling these early followers: "We don't lose our passion. Even if everything around us is chaotic, our hope is not a prisoner to circumstance. Our hope is settled, it is secure, and it gives us drive and passion." Be this kind of follower of Jesus. Some people energize you just by their presence. I like to remind myself that if I am not energized, I must not be in the presence of Jesus, because Jesus energizes everyone He encounters.

UNSEEN

"For the things we see now will soon be gone, but the things we cannot see will last forever."
2 Corinthians 4:18b

It is so easy to think that the stuff that really matters is the stuff we can observe with our eyes. The writer of this letter to the Corinthians is saying: Oops, it's the other way around. It's not material that goes on forever; it's the immaterial. It's not stuff you can buy with money; it's stuff you could never buy with money, no matter how much money you had. We know this, yet we don't practice it. My goodness, how simple life is and yet so difficult. Invest your time today in unseen things. Thankfully our words, what we say, can set a direction in the unseen. They can change people's hearts and minds. Be a blessing today in the unseen world.

JULY 26

TRAVEL COMPANION

"For the Lord your God is going with you!"
Deuteronomy 20:4a

Everybody knows that if you are going on a journey it's nice to have company, whether it's a summertime trip or the journey of life. This Old Testament passage is prophetically reminding God's people that whoever is with you and wherever you go in the natural world, God is going with you in the supernatural. You have the best traveling partner of all. Enjoy His company today.

DEFENDER

"He will fight for you against your enemies,
and he will give you victory."
Deuteronomy 20:4b

The beauty of this is the reminder that God's role in your life is not that of a casual spectator. He does not stand by as a passive, disinterested party. He actively engages to protect you, guide you, fight for you, and give you victory. He will fight for you today.

JULY 28

PERSPECTIVE

"The temptations in your life are no different from what others experience."
1 Corinthians 10:13a

It is almost humorous (if it wasn't so sad) how frequently people talk about God as if He is trying to ensnare His own people, trap His own children, or make us look foolish. God is not working against you. He is not hoping that your stupidity and weakness will be displayed. He is hoping for your redemption, forgiveness, and purity. He is working for you, not against you. So today, stop pretending like He is your enemy, and start acting like He is on your side.

EMPOWERED

"And God is faithful. He will not allow the temptation to be more than you can stand."
1 Corinthians 10:13b

God is faithful when you are not. God will always step in before you break. So if you feel like you are breaking and God is not stepping in, this is a sign that there is more strength in you. It has become an annoyance to me when I hear people say, "I can't go on," or, "I just can't do it anymore." Because clearly Scripture teaches that you can go on and you can keep going because He is with you. He will not let you break. He lives in you and His Spirit comes out of every pore of your body. Have faith: you can do it!

EXIT STRATEGY

"When you are tempted, he will show you a way out so that you can endure."
1 Corinthians 10:13c

Sometimes God stops the temptation before we break and sometimes He provides a relief valve, a way out. When God provides a way out, take it. When He gives you a window to crawl out of, do it. When He leaves a door open, walk through it. Sometimes I wonder if we are angrier at ourselves for not taking God's rescue, or at God for not "making" us do the right thing. God is your partner; you are not His robot. He created you and He gives you the ability to use your will to follow Him and love Him. Do it today. Maybe the greatest thing you can do is to take the way out He provides so you can live to fight another day. Be encouraged today. God is working for you to find a way out.

IN HIM

"I have told you all this so that you may have peace in me."
John 16:33a

Jesus gives us information that sometimes troubles us. Yet His intent is that we have peace—in Him. Two key words. If you are interpreting the world with so much negativity that your peace is gone, then insert more Jesus into your outlook. Today, take the information around you, the data you gather from all of your senses and from the use of your mind, and apply faith to it. Be at peace in Him today.

HOPE FOR AUGUST

WINNING

"Here on earth you will have many trials and sorrows. But take heart, because I have overcome the world."
John 16:33b

A song I grew up hearing included the line, "I never promised you a rose garden." Similar to the message of this song, Jesus never promised that we wouldn't have trouble. In fact, He promised that we would. So we shouldn't be shocked when life is difficult. It's par for the course, as they say. What is shocking is that we can have peace in the midst of difficulty, and He tells us why. The words you read above are a direct quote from Jesus: "I have overcome the world." He won, and He lives in you, so you win. Take heart today!

AUGUST 2

READY

"Therefore, put on every piece of God's armor…."
Ephesians 6:13a

The sentence continues, but we'll stop and ponder this today: Armor is meant for battle, and battles are meant for victories. So wherever you are, get ready for a fight. Whatever fight you are in, get ready for a victory. Maybe there's no battle in sight. Or maybe you're up to your teeth in one and victory seems impossible. Either way, we don't live by what we can see; we live by faith. Whatever you think the next 24 hours may hold, get ready for a great day by putting on every piece of God's armor.

STANDING FIRM

"...so you will be able to resist the enemy in the time of evil. Then after the battle you will still be standing firm." Ephesians 6:13b

Yesterday we read instructions to "put on the full armor of God." Now we read that the reason to do this is so we "will still be standing firm" after the battle. I remember a song from the 1980s in which the artist sings, "I'm still standing." Isn't it encouraging to reflect on how we are still standing after the countless ways the devil has tried to injure and kill us? Perhaps he tried to kill you before you were even born. He may have tried to steal your joy through childhood hardships, or urged you to take your own life during a difficult season. Yet, we are still standing. To the extent that we put on the armor of God we will be able to withstand even bigger battles. Put it on today!

ALSO KNOWN AS

"This letter is from James, a slave of God and of the Lord Jesus Christ." James 1:1a

I once heard a sermon about James called, "Things I Would Never Say about My Brother." James was the brother of Jesus. Which makes the opening sentence of his letter surprising, if not shocking. Instead of introducing himself as, "James, brother of Jesus," he instead calls himself a "slave" of his own brother, whom he calls "the Lord Jesus Christ." Sometimes it's helpful to think about ourselves and our own identity, but more often, we get better by thinking of Jesus. Think about the fact that Jesus was so holy and good that even His own family and those who surrounded Him saw His divinity. If you are a follower of Jesus, you are not following a myth or a legend. You are following God Himself. Jesus was God in the flesh and with my dying breath I will say He is my Savior and Lord. How about you?

CONSIDER

"Dear brothers and sisters, when troubles of any kind come your way, consider it an opportunity for great joy."
James 1:2

Could James really mean this? I like that he uses the word "consider." This means you are going to have to think about it, and then think about it some more. It's neither natural nor intuitive to be happy in the midst of trouble. But consider reframing your worst moments, days, and seasons—your hardships, losses, and mistakes—in the light of what Jesus has done and can do. He has a way of taking our worst moments and turning them into unlikely blessing. Be a thinker today. Contemplate finding "great joy" in your biggest problems and smallest nuisances. You will need to sift the dirt to find the gold. I think you will make your day, your week, and your life better.

ANTIDOTE

"My days fly faster than a weaver's shuttle.
They end without hope."
Job 7:6

Oh my. Don't let this be said of you. Job was lamenting and feeling sorry for himself. It's natural to feel despair when we are overwhelmed by circumstances and swept along by life's momentum, but don't be Job today. Do everything you can to get around hope, ingest hope, read hope, and talk about hope. When you live for Jesus, you have a guarantee that your days will not end without hope, but will be filled with purpose and end with joy.

SAVIOR

"God sent his Son into the world not to judge the world, but to save the world. . . ."
John 3:17a

Wow! Here's a hopeful thought. God is not trying to catch you doing the wrong thing. Jesus came as a Savior, not an executioner. If you are feeling hopeless, run to Jesus.

AUGUST 8

INVITED

"Then you will call on me and come and pray to me, and I will listen to you."
Jeremiah 29:12 (NIV)

There are three steps for us here. "Call on Me" is the first one, "come" is the second, and the third is "pray (talk) to Me." It's like knocking on a door, walking through the door, and starting a conversation. Hope happens when we know we have someone with us, seeing us, and hearing us. Think of a time when you felt completely alone, and then you talked and someone listened. It made all the difference, didn't it? Jesus is with you today and every day. Knock on the door, walk through the door, and talk to Him. He will listen to you.

ALIVE & WELL

"According to his great mercy, he has caused us to be born again to a living hope...."
I Peter 1:3b (ESV)

When we pray and sing to Jesus, together in groups or by ourselves, we are not addressing our words to a dead man, but rather to a living friend who literally gave His own life for us. He died for our sins (He didn't have a single one of His own) and came to life again, so we could figuratively do the same. We can "put to death" our own sin and accept Jesus' payment for it, and be "born again" into the living hope He created for us with His own life. If you know Jesus, bring Him up in conversation with someone today and talk about the living hope you have because of Him. He lives!

AUGUST 10

TOMORROW

"...and we rejoice in the hope of the glory of God."
Romans 5:2b (ESV)

Something about knowing that tomorrow might get better makes us happy. That's what hope does: it lifts our spirit. Today, whatever else is going on, try putting on a smile, knowing that whatever happens today, tomorrow could be better and almost certainly will be better with Jesus with you in it.

HEART GRIP

"So we do not lose heart."
2 Corinthians 4:16a (ESV)

Do you believe in the power of your words? I do. When the writer of this letter says, "So we do not lose heart," I believe he is not just telling others, but also reminding himself. Hope is something we have to grab onto with both hands. Resolve today: "I will not lose hope. I am not going to live just by what I feel or see; I'm going to live by what God says. I will not lose hope. I will not, I will not." Who can you encourage today to "not lose heart?"

AUGUST 12

UNSEEN

"For the things we see now will soon be gone, but the things we cannot see will last forever."
2 Corinthians 4:18b

This makes sense! Now we know why the writer doesn't lose heart. He is setting his focus on what cannot be shaken, spoil, or be stolen. What you have in your pocket will most certainly go away, but the hope Jesus promises is permanent. What are you holding onto that you "cannot see" today? Don't let it be bitterness or selfishness. Don't let it be sadness or anger. Let it be the hope of Jesus, and invite someone to share it with you. It is the greatest gift you could give them, the greatest gift they could receive, a gift they "cannot see [that] will last forever."

UNDESERVED

"God saved you by his grace when you believed.
And you can't take credit for this;
it is a gift from God."
Ephesians 2:8

Are you a Jesus person? Have you ever prayed and welcomed Him in? Don't take another breath without talking to Jesus and receiving His grace. Grace means you don't deserve it, but He does it anyway. That is fact. You really don't deserve it and neither do I. But He loves us and wants to save us anyway.

AUGUST 14

SURE HOPE

"For in this hope we were saved."
Romans 8:24a (NIV)

When it comes to hope, God took the first step. He sent His own Son as a good faith offering. He put His contribution on the table first. And because He did, our hope is not unfounded. We can already see and feel what He has done for us to show His love, so we have no reason to doubt what He says He will do. Be prayerful this week, will you, that friends you know will be saved into this hope? It is everything.

ENDURANCE + ENCOURAGEMENT

"...that through endurance and through the encouragement of the Scriptures we might have hope."
Romans 15:4b (ESV)

Here we find two elements that contribute to hope. One is endurance, which is our part. Don't give up, don't look back, and don't look to the left or to the right. The other is encouragement, which God gives us through His word. The Scriptures encourage us by reminding us that great men and women have gone before us and led the way. We are not traveling a path no one else has walked. Instead, we are walking in the footsteps of others who have endured. Read some of His story today. Be encouraged and endure.

AUGUST 16

GOD OF HOPE

"May the God of hope fill you with all joy and peace...."
Romans 15:13a (ESV)

God doesn't just do hope, He is the God of hope. He is the creator of it, the ruler of it, the generous giver of it. He imagined hope and He made it real. Greek mythology called hope a curse, but God owned it and said, "I am the God of hope." Do you need hope today, and "all joy and peace?" I can't think of a better place to find it than in the God of hope. Be encouraged today. Encourage others.

TAILWIND

"...so that by the power of the Holy Spirit you may abound in hope."
Romans 15:13b (ESV)

The Holy Spirit is the engine. He is the wind in your sail. People on a sailboat pay attention to which way the wind is blowing and set their sail that way. So pay attention to what God is doing and set your life that way. It's the same idea. Is there anything more beautiful than a sailboat on a windy day, with the sunshine out? Is there anything sweeter than someone who is full of hope because of something invisible the Holy Spirit is doing in them? Don't burn out your engine by trying to willpower your way through life, or get caught in the world's current and carried off course. Let the Holy Spirit fill your sails with His power and your heart with hope today.

AUGUST 18

EPICENTER

"And as Moses lifted up the bronze snake on a pole in the wilderness, so the Son of Man must be lifted up." John 3:14

There is a lot of foreshadowing in the Bible—hints on earlier pages about events we then read about in later chapters, and still more hints about what has yet to become a part of history. What matters most is keeping Jesus in the center of the entire timeline. This Scripture reminds us that God telegraphed over decades and centuries, to generation after generation, that He was going to send a Savior. Now He is telegraphing that He is coming again. Whatever is going on in your life today, keep Jesus at the center of it. He did come and He is coming again. Don't let fear and worry today overshadow the truth of what He has done in the past and the promise of what He will do in the future.

EVERYONE

"so that everyone who believes in him...."
John 3:15

Everyone means everyone. In a world filled with divisions, disagreements, and diversity, Jesus is a reconciler, a fixer, someone who welds people together instead of tearing them apart. He mends ripped places. Who are you separated from today? What relationship is "beyond repair?" Jesus is for everyone—not just the "good" people, but the rest of us, too. This color and that color, that group and this group. "Everyone who believes." I'm glad I fit into the category of everyone. So do you, by the way.

REVERSAL

"And the judgment is based on this fact: God's light came into the world, but people loved the darkness more than the light...."
John 3:19a

In some translations the word "fact" is translated "verdict." Verdict is a legal term. It means a decision passed down by a judge, which must then be honored and accepted (or appealed) by others. The Bible refers to God as the righteous judge. Although He has not yet rendered a sentence, it's obvious what the verdict will be for many. We love our mess more than we love His message. We love our garbage more than we love His cleansing. Thankfully, we are just one change of mind away from a different life. It only takes a moment. Why not this moment? Set aside the darkness in your life and love the light. Love Jesus.

RECEIVE

"And Jesus added, 'The Son of Man is Lord, even over the Sabbath.'"
Luke 6:5

Jesus is saying that He created His rules to be a blessing to us, not a prison. The Sabbath is a sweet gift He gave us. Too often we reject the gift, or receive it as a burden with a spirit of obligation rather than with gratitude for the blessing it is. Don't be weighed down by any gift God gives you. Receive it in the spirit in which it is given: for your benefit so you can fully live the significant, unique life He planned specifically for you.

AUGUST 22

DAY BY DAY

"And there will be strange signs in the sun, moon, and stars. And here on earth the nations will be in turmoil, perplexed by the roaring seas and strange tides." Luke 21:25

Here Jesus is talking about earth's last days. He clearly knows the specifics, but His description is vague enough that it is difficult for us to know whether these days are happening now or still in the future. One thing we can know beyond a doubt: we are definitely in the process of spending our days. I'm approaching 18,000 days of being alive and I would be a fool to assume even one more day is guaranteed. Whatever perplexity and struggle is going on, whatever the world is doing and whatever seas are roaring, walk with Jesus just for today. And then walk with Him again tomorrow.

HONOR

"so that everyone will honor the Son...."
John 5:23a

Most of us are shy about demanding or requesting honor. Jesus was not so shy. It's almost immodest how He talks about Himself. He wants to hold a place of honor in your life and He is not afraid to ask for it. Second place may be good enough for others, but He refuses it. He wants to matter and be important to you—not be an afterthought or someone you squeeze into your day. Take a deep breath today and figure out how you can invite Jesus into all of your appointments and all of your day. I don't think you will be sorry.

AUGUST 24

PARADIGM SHIFT

"But don't be so concerned about perishable things like food. Spend your energy seeking the eternal life...."
John 6:27

Most of life is temporary. I'll say it again: most of life is temporary. It only seems permanent. The flowers you're looking at right now, as beautiful as they are, are almost gone. The sun, as long as it has been here, will someday stop shining. So the question is, how can we live with urgency and happiness? The answer is to live for eternity. Whatever happens today, if you know Jesus, your "tomorrow" will be sweet.

DON'T & DO

"Don't let your hearts be troubled. Trust in God, and trust also in me."
John 14:1

The first part of this verse tells us not to allow our hearts to be troubled—fearful or worried. The second part tells us to definitely allow trust in God. And even better yet, trust in Jesus. This is how we keep fear out. It's like a room that is already occupied. "Fear, you cannot stay here. Jesus already has occupancy." Let Him in and let Him have the keys. Let Him have his way. Trust Him.

AUGUST 26

LISTEN

"Then Jesus called to the crowd to come and hear. 'Listen,' he said, 'and try to understand.'"
Matthew 15:10

It's shocking to me how many people want to understand—or think they already do—without listening. There is a sequence to life. You're not going to "get it" until you listen. I don't think we live in a listening world. We live in an opinion world. Turn off your microphone and turn up your hearing aid. Listen first...and then try to understand.

ADDITIVES

"Their worship is a farce, for they teach man-made ideas as commands from God."
Matthew 15:9

Please forgive me for being repetitive, but so much of what we call "Christianity" is additions prescribed by well-intentioned followers. Every morning, say Jesus' name out loud and focus on Him. When considering instruction, be discerning about what is "bonus material" from a particular church or well-meaning person. Truly following Jesus is all about Jesus all the time.

AUGUST 28

PERMISSION

"He replied, 'You are permitted to understand the secrets of the Kingdom of Heaven but others are not.'"
Matthew 13:11

When God rolled out the Jesus chapter of His plan for the world and eternity, He started with a core group. What happened next? Exactly what happens today: some accept and embrace it; others reject it and are disinterested. If you already know the joy of life with Jesus, don't be shocked that some people don't want the secret. It has been this way since the beginning. God has chosen you to be a megaphone to a hard-of-hearing world. Share the secret indiscriminately today. Not all may want it or be willing to hear it, but everyone needs it.

ADDED

"But seek first the kingdom of God and his righteousness, and all these things will be added to you."
Matthew 6:33 (ESV)

Do you wonder what "all these things" encompasses? If I reflect on the various seasons and areas of my life, I see lots of days where I could have used a little more of "all these things." But when I ask the question, "Has God added more to me than I could ever expect?" the answer is always a resounding yes. Yes, yes, yes, and a thousand times yes. Thankfully, He is and blesses me with better than I deserve. I suspect it is the same for you too. What has God added to your life? Walk like a grateful person today, seeking Him first.

SUPERWORDS

*"Gracious words are like a honeycomb,
sweetness to the soul and health to the body."*
Proverbs 16:24 (ESV)

Wow! Don't you just want to read that again? Like your favorite candy, gracious words go right to the sweet spot on your palate and you can't help but savor them. But unlike candy, gracious words are more than just sweet: they are health to the body. Did you know honey is actually rich in antioxidants? It may taste sweet, but it helps you like vegetables. In the same way, gracious words do your body good. Why not give some gracious words to people today? Be sure to savor the ones that others give to you. There is a lot of sour out there; let's keep giving the sweet.

SOFT-SPOKEN

"A soft answer turns away wrath,
but a harsh word stirs up anger."
Proverbs 15:1 (ESV)

I often say this verse to myself. I try to come up with "soft answers." It's interesting how the writer contrasts a soft answer with a harsh word. It is not just an answer that can be harsh; it can be even shorter: as simple as a word. People really are sensitized to every word we say—including ourselves. (Notice the writer doesn't specify who is getting angry: the one speaking the harsh words, the one receiving them, or both.) So be thoughtful today when you speak, and try to extract all of the harsh words whenever possible. It will be a blessing to both you and others.

SEPTEMBER

SELF-EDIT

"Don't use foul or abusive language. Let everything you say be good and helpful, so that your words will be an encouragement to those who hear them."
Ephesians 4:29

We live in a "talk" culture, don't we? And the talk on our radios, televisions, and other media has a way of souring not just our own spirit, but those around us as well. Speaking for myself, unless I make a focused effort to do otherwise, it is easy to be a reflection of the talk that surrounds me. Let's agree today, just for one day, to be conduits of good, helpful, and encouraging words. If we catch ourselves being discouraged or discouraging, let's put an eraser to the moment and begin again.

SEPTEMBER 2

PEP TALK

"So encourage each other and build each other up, just as you are already doing."
1 Thessalonians 5:11

What a compliment the writer was giving this early church! He was saying, "You are doing it! Keep on going!" Encouraging and building. Encouraging can feel empty by itself if not accompanied by action or grounded in relevance. Clearly, these people were not empty; what they were saying and doing was effective. Let's you and I be these people today. Say the words that give people energy and do the things that build people up.

BE HAPPY

"Always be joyful."
1 Thessalonians 5:16

Sometimes there is not much to be happy about. Yet the instruction here is "always." This is our cue to get out our microscope and start looking for something within our situation that might be a nugget of gold. Happy people, rejoicing people, are people who don't have everything perfect, but who can find something precious in the middle of whatever they are experiencing. Be that kind of person today.

SEPTEMBER 4

ALWAYS | NEVER | ALL

"Always be joyful. Never stop praying. Be thankful in all circumstances, for this is God's will for you who belong to Christ Jesus."
1 Thessalonians 5:16-18

Jesus is never separated from your dilemmas. He is never separated from your dreams. In all circumstances, if you are moving forward you are going to be striving. If you are striving you are going to get hurt. If you are hurt, you are going to be hesitant about taking more steps. But in it all, good or bad, Jesus is with you. If you cannot walk, let Him carry you. Get happy. Rejoice always in Jesus Christ.

RIGHT TRACK

"This is the day the Lord has made."
Psalm 118:24a

Most folks are pretty good at keeping track of the offenses they experience. But too many of us are sloppy about the way we keep track of what the Lord has done, even today. The fact that you are here, breathing and upright, the fact that you are a part of one more 24-hour segment, is evidence God is working. Can you imagine if your children only remembered your corrections and not your caress or your gifts? Don't be that way with your Creator. Jesus loves you. Today He wants to do something special through you, in you. Now that's something to keep track of.

SEPTEMBER 6

REAL LOVE

"You love him even though you have never seen him. Though you do not see him now, you trust him...."
1 Peter 1:8a

It is kind of odd, isn't it, how we talk about Jesus sometimes? I have to be reminded that I have never seen Him with my eyes. He seems so intimate to me, so real, so personal. Peter reminds us we are blessed because we have the faith to believe in something we cannot see. Be proud of yourself today.

YET

"Even though the fig trees have no blossoms, and there are no grapes on the vines; even though the olive crop fails, and the fields lie empty and barren; even though the flocks die in the fields, and the cattle barns are empty, yet I will rejoice in the LORD!"
Habakkuk 3:17-18a

All I can say about this verse is that I am working on it. Not there yet. How about you?

SEPTEMBER 8

MENTAL MATH

"When anxiety was great within me,
your consolation brought me joy."
Psalm 94:19 (NIV)

This is a math problem, isn't it? When anxiety was adding up, the writer went on trying to multiply his joy. Don't let anxiety subtract from your joy as it gains momentum and accumulates. God's consolation—redirection of what you're thinking about and meditating on—will bring you joy. Focus on what is left and not what is lost. Focus on what is ahead and not on what was behind. When you nail this, when you can perfect this, you have gained a valuable skill.

BY NAME

"You haven't done this before. Ask, using my name, and you will receive, and you will have abundant joy."
John 16:24

Surely the men to whom Jesus gives this instruction had prayed. But apparently they had prayed to the Father and not in Jesus' name. When I pray today, I definitely use Jesus' name. Perhaps you most often begin your prayers with "Heavenly Father," or another name for God that feels most comfortable or meaningful to you. I encourage you to begin praying in the name of Jesus. Little keys open big doors. Little hinges swing big gates open. This little name, the name of Jesus, carpenter from Nazareth, means something big in the spiritual world.

BUSINESS

"I have seen the business that God has given to the children of man to be busy with."
Ecclesiastes 3:10 (ESV)

This statement comes from one of the wisest men who ever lived, who was also very disillusioned with what he saw in the world around him. I want to question the premise. Certainly God has given us business or assignments to do. But God hasn't given you busyness to merely "be busy with." Today let's be about His business, not about our busyness. There is a radical difference.

PEACE

"And the peace I give is a gift the world cannot give. So don't be troubled or afraid."
John 14:27b

Have you ever thought about different kinds of peace? The peace talked about here is better than any peace you and I can give each other, or that might come from a beautiful piece of music or art or a visit to the spa or a setting in nature. This is Jesus' peace. It's like He's loaning us His spirit. Jesus tells us His peace is definitely not the same brand as the world's version of peace. What the world has is temporary and conditional. What Jesus has—and freely gives us in generous measure—is permanent and unconditional. Enjoy His peace today.

SEPTEMBER 12

SEASONS

"For everything there is a season..."
Ecclesiastes 3:1a

I often find myself wishing God would edit life differently. Wouldn't it be wonderful if we only had sunshine and never rain? Or always summer and never winter? But when I stop and think about it, I realize that type of season has a name, too: we call it drought. Don't wish for drought. Instead, enjoy every season, for every season has a purpose. We don't want drought; we want lush and fruitful lives.

BE STILL

"Be still, and know that I am God!"
Psalm 46:10a

There are some things you cannot know when you are running around. There are some sensations you will never have if you are hustling and bustling. Be still, slow down, take a breath, pause, reflect, and know that God is on the throne.

SEPTEMBER 14

IN DUE SEASON

"And let us not grow weary of doing good, for in due season we will reap, if we do not give up."
Galatians 6:9 (ESV)

The phrase here that stands out to me today is, "in due season." I wish I was in charge of seasons—which ones, when they come, and how long they last. Instead, God is in charge of seasons. And I am in charge of faithfulness, perseverance, and not giving up. At least, I am for my life. Who is in charge of it for yours?

IDLENESS

"Yet we hear that some of you are living idle lives..."
2 Thessalonians 3:11a

Idleness, I think, is a particular temptation in today's culture. For some, it is tempting because of prosperity. For others, because of poverty. Whatever the excuse, put meaning into your day today. God gave us one day to rest, not seven. And even that one day is for intentional rest, not careless indolence. One day to reflect and give Him your full attention. Whether today is a rest day or work day for you, don't be idle; be impactful.

9-1-1

"Come quickly, Lord, and answer me,
for my depression deepens...."
Psalm 143:7a

Wow. I think I have prayed this prayer. "Answer me, God, because I don't think I can keep going." I am not sure God always answers that prayer in the way we expect Him to, but I know He helps us when we ask Him. He lifts my spirit when it has fallen, or keeps it from falling in the first place. Sometimes He answers through the Holy Spirit, sometimes through His word, sometimes He sends a friend to encourage. It is a lie when we say we "can't go on," because we certainly can. We just can't go on without help from Jesus. So ask for help today.

TRUST

"Let me hear of your unfailing love each morning, for I am trusting you. Show me where to walk, for I give myself to you."
Psalm 143:8b

Wonderful, wonderful, wonderful. I love the trust and transparency expressed here, and the picture it brings to mind. Doesn't it sound like the relationship between a loving parent and trusting child? What child doesn't need to hear every day that he or she is loved? And what child doesn't need a parent guiding and showing him how to navigate life? From the day we are born to the day our earthly lives end, this is who God is to us, what He wants to do for us, and how He wants us to be in relationship with Him. Make this verse your prayer to Him today.

DILIGENCE

"The plans of the diligent lead surely to abundance...."
Proverbs 21:5a (ESV)

It's discouraging sometimes, isn't it, how often God asks us to be participants in our own life? Don't you just wish He would just make us robots who simply do what He wants us to do? Well, maybe not. Diligence is not automatic; it is a choice and an action. And abundance is not an accident; it is a result. God's part is His goodness and faithfulness. Our part is diligence. And the Bible says that diligence will lead to abundance. My prayer today is that you will have an abundant life because of how good God is and how diligent you are.

TELL & SHOW

"And since you know that he cares,
let your language show it."
James 5:12a (MSG)

Sometimes we use our words to talk about what we want to change. Sometimes we talk about things we are glad haven't changed. I am glad God has not changed. I am glad He is still faithful, still loving, and still kind. I am glad He is still the way, the truth, and the life. Today, instead of talking about what you would like Jesus to do for you, let your words talk about what He has already done for you.

DETAILS

"Go out and stand before me
on the mountain..."
1 Kings 19:11a

Sometimes God asks us to do things that seem meaningless, like this instruction about where He would like the prophet Isaiah to stand. But in the next sentence, we find out the Lord "passed by" the very spot where Isaiah was standing. Perhaps the small instruction God is giving you right now is preceding a big appearance by Him. Let's do as He asks today, and see what happens next.

PATTERNS

"Do not conform to the pattern of this world...."
Romans 12:2a (NIV)

This world has a pattern. Can you see it? If not, take a closer look around you today and think about what you see. My son makes clothes, and learned very quickly that patterns—the measurements and map for each item—are everything. If you follow the pattern, you get the same result every time. And if the pattern is off, the garment will be also. The same is true for the "pattern" of this world. If you follow it, you'll become what the world wants you to become. Do you like the pattern you see? And the way it shapes those who follow it? Today, choose not to follow the pattern of this world. Pick a better one. I recommend following Jesus.

MINDFUL

"...But be transformed by the renewing of your mind."
Romans 12:2b

Your brain is not your mind. Your brain is an organ in your head. Your mind is all of the life, experience, and wisdom that you have gathered in your brain. Be transformed by the wisdom, insight, and whisper of the Holy Spirit. You can do it! You don't have to do the same thing today that you did yesterday or last year. You are not a bear that instinctively has to hibernate or a bird that has to fly south. You are a child of the living God.

SEPTEMBER 23

EN ROUTE

"As Jesus and his disciples continued on their way...."
Luke 10:38a

I love that things can happen when we are "on our way." And that Jesus is right there with us when they do. Significant experiences. Conversations. Breakthroughs. Today you are on your way to somewhere. You haven't yet reached your destination, and may in fact be somewhere very different than you intended. But just as He was with His disciples, Jesus is with you while you are on your way. Don't be thrown off by distractions or interruptions (though Jesus is with you in those as well). Instead, listen for His footsteps alongside you and His voice in your ear.

ROOTS

"They are like trees planted along the riverbank, bearing fruit each season. Their leaves never wither, and they prosper in all they do."
Psalm 1:3

This psalm is reflecting on the type of person who has his or her roots near an unending source, and whose branches are a blessing to everyone around. Today, do not worry about the fruit; worry about the source. Right now, say a 60-second prayer. It does not have to be long or detailed. Just put your roots into Jesus. His stream never runs dry.

WEALTH

"Honor the Lord with your wealth...."
Proverbs 3:9a

If you think about it, wherever we place our wealth is also where we place our honor. The key word in this little sentence is "Lord." A lord is someone who is in charge, the boss, a savior. This instruction is saying, use your wealth to honor Jesus. Not just your income, but your wealth. Your income is what people would pay you in a transaction; your wealth is everything you own and have accumulated—your house, your car, your savings, your retirement, and of course your income. Know this: right now you are using your wealth to honor something or someone. If you are like most people, you are using it to honor yourself. Is that working for you? Try honoring Jesus with your wealth—all of it—and see the difference it makes.

BEST

"...and with the best part of everything you produce. Then he will fill your barns with grain, and your vats will overflow with good wine."
Proverbs 3:9b-10

The first part of this sentence says, "Honor the Lord with your wealth"—everything you already have. Today we're looking at the income part of the sentence and the equation. Everything you are working for right now is part of a sowing-and-reaping, investing-and-earning equation. Take not the last little bit, but the first and best, and use it to produce more happiness and blessing in your life. This seems counterintuitive to some, but makes a lot of sense to others. If you're a grower, you do not eat all of your seed. You plant your seeds, tend the plants that grow, and then eat the fruit they produce. When you take the first fruit and plant it again, all the seeds inside of it are getting ready to give you even more. Think about it today. Better yet, do it.

GIVE

"Give, and you will receive." Luke 6:38a

This often poses a dilemma for people. The most altruistic feel it somehow cheapens their giving if they receive something in return. To others it sounds like a scam, too good to be true. And frankly, sometimes those who cite this verse are more interested in their own gain.

Regardless of how we may think or feel about the idea, it's an instruction God put in His word to us. His instructions are always for our benefit. If you are not yet a giver (and, consequently, a receiver), I encourage you to start with a small amount and give over a period of time without telling anyone else. Keep track of what you give, and see if God rips you off. Yes, it requires trust on the front end. But if God doesn't take care of you, never give another cent. I think you will be more generous at the end of your experiment. God is in no one's debt.

SEPTEMBER 28

FULL CIRCLE

"Your gift will return to you in full—pressed down, shaken together to make room for more, running over, and poured into your lap. The amount you give will determine the amount you get back."
Luke 6:38b

On the heels of yesterday's thought, these sentences say the same thing a whole lot more emphatically. In essence, Luke is saying, "I'm not talking about diminishing returns here. This really happens!" Compelling, isn't it? I became a giver years ago and have been increasing my generosity ever since. The more I trust God with my money, the more money I have to trust Him with, and it gets a virtuous cycle going. Wouldn't it be nice to be in a virtuous cycle and not a vicious one? Start a good cycle right now. Find where God is at work and invest in it today.

PROVISION

"So don't worry about these things, saying, 'What will we eat?'"
Matthew 6:31a

Certainly when we look around, not everybody has what they want. But it is remarkable how we always seem to get what we need. The government tells us 64 percent of the kids in our public schools need free and reduced lunch, so we gather and create programs and make sure they will not go hungry. In fact, we have been so successful that our kids are obese. Our idea of "poverty" today is pretty different than what it looked like generations ago. Do not let worry steal your joy. God has a way of getting people something to eat—including you and even others through you. Be a conduit for generosity today.

SEPTEMBER 30

SUDDENLY

"Suddenly, there was a sound from heaven like the roaring of a mighty windstorm, and it filled the house where they were sitting." Acts 2:2

Whenever you hear the word "suddenly," it is full of excitement. Not everything that happens suddenly is good, but it does indicate a significant change has happened. Often the Holy Spirit seems shy. He is continuously working—convicting, lifting, encouraging—invisibly and imperceptibly in so many ways and places throughout our world. But periodically, there are also those "suddenly" moments when He shows himself, when the sound and the sense of Him fills our home and changes the atmosphere. You can be certain He is there all the time, even when you're unaware. But it sure is nice to sense His power every so often. Watch and listen today for the move of the Holy Spirit in your home.

HOPE FOR

OCTOBER

COMFORTER

"And I will pray (to) the Father, and he shall give you another Comforter, that he may abide with you forever;"
John 14:16 (KJV)

There is so much here. Jesus saw Himself as a Comforter and now He is telling His followers that the Father will send another Comforter like Him to live in their hearts forever. I could not be more thankful for any truth than I am for this one. Jesus and His Spirit have made a place in my heart. Have they made a place in yours? Put out the welcome mat today for the Comforter to abide in you.

SIGNED

"For the Spirit of God has made me, and the breath of the Almighty gives me life."
Job 33:4

You were designed, sketched out, assembled, created, and then animated. Design indicates forethought and artistry. Assembly shows careful craftsmanship. The breath, the animation of God, means energy and power. All three of these abide in you and live in you. Walk with your head up today. You bear the signature of the Master.

OCTOBER 3

LIFE

"...the Spirit gives life."
2 Corinthians 3:6b

Scientists and doctors are interested when someone takes his last breath, or her first. They study death and life. They want to know what happens when our breath leaves us. They know life is not sustained without breath, which is why machines must "breathe for" people who are unable to breathe on their own. When breath leaves your body, you weigh pretty much the same. So whatever the Holy Spirit has put in you, it doesn't weigh anything. But it means everything. You have been given LIFE. Don't take it for granted and certainly don't waste it. Live life to the fullest today.

MOVED

"...those prophets were moved by the Holy Spirit, and they spoke from God."
2 Peter 1:21b

Lots of people say too much when they have imbibed too many "spirits." Jack Daniels has caused plenty of arguments. The spirits this world lives on will give you words that hurt and destroy. But holy men, set-apart women, people who live differently, speak as they are moved by the Holy Spirit, not just the spirit of this world. Be careful what induces you to say things. Let it not be temper, fear, alcohol, or pain. Make what you say be holy, good, uplifting, and set apart. Sounds difficult, doesn't it? On your own, it might be. Let the Holy Spirit be the One who moves you and speaks through you.

OCTOBER 5

ARMED

"Put on salvation as your helmet, and take the sword of the Spirit, which is the word of God."
Ephesians 6:17

The helmet protects your head, the control tower of your body. Being saved by what Jesus did on the cross protects the control tower of your life. But the real weapon is not your salvation; it is what God has spoken over you and over the place where you live. God has promises and principles for you. Don't treat them casually. Read His word; it gives you weapons to defend against the enemy, win victories, and take new territory. You do not have to keep living the way you have been living. Life gets better from here.

PRESENCE

"You will show me the way of life, granting me the joy of your presence and the pleasures of living with you forever."
Psalm 16:11

Don't you love poets? They express thoughts so succinctly in such beautiful language. Here the psalmist reminds us that whenever we're with Jesus and the Father, we have a higher level of joy. Being with Him and serving Him is one pleasure after another—not necessarily easy, but a pleasure. He is so good to us. Thank Him today for His presence. I hope you haven't been around Him so long that you've forgotten what a pleasure it is.

OCTOBER 7

WISDOM

"Joyful is the person who finds wisdom,
the one who gains understanding."
Proverbs 3:13

Wisdom isn't just information or data. It is learning, understanding, and then using what you know to create a better life for yourself and others. You know someone is wise when they become a little more like Jesus every day. Their life doesn't necessarily become easier, but their direction is steady. Do you consider yourself wise? If not, why not? If you're looking to be happy, go where the wisdom is. Find wisdom and you'll find joy.

EXCEPTIONAL

"But the servant of the Lord must not strive,
but must be gentle toward all men,
apt to teach, suffering the evil,"
2 Timothy 2:24 (GNV)

This is not easy. It tells us not to strive, but other portions of Scripture tell us not to bury our talents either. It seems like Paul is speaking to our motives. What are we motivated by? Is it to hurt people or to build people? Is it for self or for others? We live in a "selfie" world. If you can be about others and make your goals more altruistic, you will be the exception and not the rule. And you really are exceptional aren't you? I believe so. Live that way today.

Q & A

"And put away foolish and unlearned questions, knowing that they engender strife."
2 Timothy 2:23 (GNV)

Everybody is looking for the right answers, but Paul is teaching his protégé that asking the right questions is the key. You learn a lot more by asking questions than by arguing about what you think you already know. Today, let your prayers be questions. Ask the Holy Spirit questions, and see what answers He leads you to. It's an exciting life; try it.

EXTINGUISH

"Fire goes out without wood, and quarrels disappear when gossip stops."
Proverbs 26:20

The writer of the wisdom book is saying, stop feeding the negative. If you don't want something remembered, stop talking about it. If you don't want it to be important, stop speaking it into existence. Do you remember that your words create your atmosphere? Surround yourself with worship music and positive conversation today. Edit yourself. I'm going to try it. This won't be easy, but it will be positive.

BEAUTIFUL

"How beautiful are the feet of messengers who bring good news!"
Romans 10:15b

In a walking culture like the first century, the feet were always dirty, always unclean. Even today in many cultures around the world, to touch someone's feet is an insult. In some cultures, if you cross your legs as gentleman and turn your feet towards someone, it is an insult. But the writer of Romans is telling us that even the dirtiest part of someone who is bringing good news is appreciated. I like that. You might not be perfect, but when you carry the love of Jesus with you, you are better received than if you're carrying only your own message. Carry on, messenger. Lead with your Jesus story; share it with someone today.

FRUIT

"But the Holy Spirit produces this kind of fruit in our lives: love, joy, peace, patience, kindness, goodness, faithfulness,"
Galatians 5:22

Let's focus on the "but." Whenever you see that word, you know a transition is happening. The sentences before this one are talking about negative fruit. When we follow our own impulses, our lives can fill up with negative consequences, can't they? You don't even have to think hard to come up with examples. But all the positive results in your life come from what the Holy Spirit is doing. Give the Holy Spirit a green light today.

OCTOBER 13

PRAYER

"Never stop praying."
1 Thessalonians 5:17

How do we do this? I have an internal dialogue going on in my head constantly. Often it's complaining or wishing or wondering or thinking. Do you do this, too? Direct it toward Jesus; let it be a prayer today.

LIFE OR DEATH

"The tongue can bring death or life; those who love to talk will reap the consequences."
Proverbs 18:21

We may lament what others say to us or around us, but we are in charge of—and responsible for—our own words. My mouth has gotten me into so much trouble. It's a constant source of repentance for me. What I speak positively to lives and thrives. What I complain to and curse dies. It's just that simple. Speak life today.

OCTOBER 15

SECURITY

"Riches won't help on the day of judgment, but right living can save you from death."
Proverbs 11:4

Some days are like a hurricane. Everything changes and there is just no winning. Have you had a few of those? When they happen, money can't help. Steve Jobs died of cancer. It doesn't matter that he helped create the modern world. It doesn't matter that he was a multi-billionaire. His wealth couldn't fix the chaos going on around him or in his body. That's just one example. Righteousness solves not just temporary problems, but eternal ones. Don't measure your security by your bank account or employment status. How are you with Jesus? That's what matters most.

PROPERTY RIGHTS

"The earth is the Lord's, and everything in it. The world and all its people belong to him."
Psalm 24:1

Have you ever been to an embassy? The rule is this: the embassy property is the property of the sponsoring country. When you walk into the Irish embassy in Washington D.C. you are actually walking on territory owned by Ireland. The same is true for our American embassy in Russia. This whole globe is an outpost of the Kingdom. You are standing on dirt that belongs to the Father. The earth was bought back by His Son Jesus and wants to be ruled by the Holy Spirit. It's a cool picture, isn't it? Let it change the way you walk through your day.

OCTOBER 17

ENOUGH

"Give me just enough to satisfy my needs. For if I grow rich, I may deny you and say, 'Who is the Lord?' And if I am too poor, I may steal and thus insult God's holy name."
Proverbs 30:8b-9

How much wisdom and control does it take to pray that prayer? To pray, "God, You know how much I can take before I get self-reliant. So don't give me so much that I will forget You." I dare you to pray that prayer today. That God would give you enough that you can be generous and helpful to others and the work of God. But not give you so much that you forget who He is. Lots of people do forget. Don't be that guy or girl.

MADE

"The rich and poor have this in common:
The Lord made them both."
Proverbs 22:2

I once heard someone say that not everyone is a child of God. I believe this is true, but had not thought of it before. Everyone is created by God, but not everyone wants to be a part of His family. Rich or poor, a bank balance status has nothing to do with whether or not God made you. And He loves you no matter what category you are in. We don't choose whether or not He made us or loves us; He did and He does. The choice we make is whether or not to be part of His family. Decide today to partner with Him in your poverty and in your wealth. Be a child of God and not just His creation.

OCTOBER 19

HUMILITY

"Pride leads to disgrace,
but with humility comes wisdom."
Proverbs 11:2

Disgrace or wisdom. It seems like an easy choice, doesn't it? It's crazy how often we pick pride. Pride is defensive, pride makes excuses, and pride assumes it is always somebody else's fault. Don't be that guy. Don't be that girl. Wisdom is knowing you are not perfect, you can't be perfect, and you are going to make mistakes. Humility is admitting your mistakes and moving forward. Today is a new day. Don't be a prisoner to yesterday's mistakes, today's pride, or tomorrow's fears. Choose humility and wisdom today.

TRIFECTA

"True humility and fear of the Lord lead to riches, honor, and long life."
Proverbs 22:4

What a nice trio this is. Wealth is income, honor is respect, and life is the thing that bubbles up inside you when you wake up in the morning. And what does the writer say leads to all of these? Humility and a genuine respect for Jesus. Not scaredy-cat fear, but respect fear. Knowing our place, and knowing God is in His place: the place of honor.

OCTOBER 21

LEGACY

"The godly walk with integrity;
blessed are their children who follow them."
Proverbs 20:7

It's probably too late for us to live blameless lives, but we can start over today. You may not see all of the blessing, but your children will. We live with our consequences, but our children live with our legacy. Righteousness starts with forgiveness and repentance. So this morning, start your day with these. Ask Jesus (and anyone else you need to) for forgiveness, and walk better, straighter, and stronger today.

PARTNERS

"An employer who hires a fool or a bystander is like an archer who shoots at random."
Proverbs 26:10

This is a statement about partnerships. It basically says, be careful who you partner with. Some of the biggest mistakes of my life have nothing to do with what I have done, but rather with what people have done in my name. Aren't you grateful God partners with you? Now we have to be careful who we connect ourselves to. Who we work with and for, and who works for us. If you're a follower of Jesus, you represent God Himself. And those with whom you partner represent you on some level. Be thoughtful about it today.

OCTOBER 23

AUTHORITY

"I tell you the truth, slaves are not greater than their master. Nor is the messenger more important than the one who sends the message."
John 13:16

Jesus had a keen sense of authority. He made no secret of the fact that He had been sent by His Father and was accountable to Him. In fact, He said the very words He spoke were commanded by God (John 12:49-50). Whose authority are you under right now? Are you uncomfortable with it? If Jesus could sit under authority, can you? You're His follower. Let's try to be honoring and respectful of those under whose authority God has placed us. It might be a challenge, but I believe it will be fruitful.

POISON

"Do not judge others, and you will not be judged. For you will be treated as you treat others...."
Matthew 7:1-2a

We are called to be discerning—observant and thoughtful. Judgment, on the other hand, assumes a higher level of authority, which this writer discourages. In our talk-saturated culture, we have become comfortable passing judgment on others. May I caution you? Be afraid of this trend not just for what it does to others, but for what it can do to you and your soul. There is something about poison that jeopardizes not only those for whom it is intended, but the hands that hold it as well. Your judgment can be poison to you and others, so handle it with care. Better yet, don't handle it at all.

OCTOBER 25

OWN

"And why worry about a speck in your friend's eye when you have a log in your own?"
Luke 6:41

You've probably heard or read this one before. Even not-religious people are familiar with this rhetorical question Jesus asked. The sliver in someone else's eye may be obvious to me, but the sliver in my own eye is equally obvious to others. Which one is my responsibility? According to Jesus, I'm not to get involved with "fixing" someone else's problem until I have tended to my own. We are responsible for our own repentance, not others'. Today, take a look inside and start there.

PEACEMAKERS

"God blesses those who work for peace, for they will be called the children of God."
Matthew 5:9

Pay attention today. What do you see and hear as you scan the headlines, browse the channels, and tune in to the discussions around you? I think you'll notice this world needs peacemakers. That's who Jesus people are. When other people are yelling, we whisper. When other people are accusing, we encourage. When other people give up, we go in. Are you a Jesus girl? Are you a Jesus guy? Let's act like it today by working for peace.

OCTOBER 27

VALUE

"Look at the birds. They don't plant or harvest or store food in barns, for your heavenly Father feeds them. And aren't you far more valuable to him than they are?"
Matthew 6:26

This one might be problematic for animal activists. Jesus is saying you are more valuable than a bird. You have a soul. You will live forever. So yes, you are more valuable than the most beautiful bird that flies through the air or sings in the sunshine. And yet, God is meticulous and loving toward that bird and all of its kind. How does that make you feel about how He must feel about you? It's wonderful to be loved like that, isn't it? Remember today how valuable you are and how much you are loved.

MERCY

"All right, but let the one who has never sinned throw the first stone!"
John 8:7b

Here is another famous Jesus quote. I'll let you figure out whether or not this qualifies you to take on the sinners around you. I, for one, am disqualified. I am, however, qualified as a Jesus person to bring life to sinners, to lift them out of dust and depravity. Be a bearer of good news today, not bad news. As the only one who had never sinned, Jesus could have cast a stone at the woman who had been accused. But He didn't. Instead, He told her what He would tell every imperfect one of us today: "Go and sin no more" (John 8:11).

OCTOBER 29

COMPASSION

"If someone has enough money to live well and sees a brother or sister in need but shows no compassion—how can God's love be in that person?"
1 John 3:17

Jesus is asking a rhetorical question, as the rabbis of that day would often do. He is pointing out a quandary: "How can God give to you, yet you're not generous?" Let's do an experiment. Today, look for a need and meet it. Give to someone by a freeway off-ramp who is holding a sign. Don't worry about their worthiness to receive; worry about your worthiness to give. Look for a mom with little kids and buy their lunch. Don't worry about her ability to care for her children; worry about your ability to show the love of Jesus. It will be a fun experiment, I promise.

BELIEVE

"Believe in the Lord your God, and you will be able to stand firm. Believe in his prophets, and you will succeed."
2 Chronicles 20:20b

Your beliefs are the root system of your life. I'll say it again: your beliefs are the root system. They are the part beneath the visible surface that goes deep down and protects you against oncoming storms. These roots secure you so you don't get blown over. And they also go deep to get water and nourishment. When you believe in God, you are becoming a deeper person. You are becoming more invincible to high winds and less susceptible to drought. Be proud of your beliefs today. Don't let cynicism and skepticism all around you steal your enthusiasm for your faith. Believe in Jesus today, and let it be known.

OCTOBER 31

GOD

"God is not a man, so he does not lie. He is not human, so he does not change his mind. Has he ever spoken and failed to act? Has he ever promised and not carried it through?"
Numbers 23:19

Have you ever noticed how movie-makers try to make people seem god-like and God seem like people? I remember the Academy Award-winning movie *Gandhi* decades ago. They made him seem like the messiah, and yet so many people want God to seem like an ordinary guy. Today, know this: God is not a man; He does not lie. He is not trying to trick you or manipulate you. He loves you and He is constant in that love. Trust Him today like you have never trusted anyone.

NOVEMBER

NOVEMBER 1

COMMANDER

"Many were possessed by demons; and the demons came out at his command...."
Luke 4:41

It's hard to know how much of the bizarre and "dark" behavior of this world is fueled by demonism. It's not hard, however, to know what or who can solve it. Many people have problems, and Jesus can deliver them all. That's the overarching principle. Whether the struggle is despair and anxiety, or a genuinely evil spirit, in the name of Jesus face it head-on today with confidence.

LOVE DOES

"But while knowledge makes us feel important, it is love that strengthens the church."
1 Corinthians 8:1b

Isn't this wonderful? It's good to have information about Scripture and matters of the divine. But it is sweet, satisfying, and impactful to have love radiating from you. Today, take in a little bit of information from your Bible. And pour out a whole bunch of love on the people in your world. Smile, speak a kind word, be a helper, give some grace. Will you do it with me?

NOVEMBER 3

RANSOMED

"God paid a high price for you,
so don't be enslaved by the world."
1 Corinthians 7:23

Ralph Waldo Emerson taught us about the importance of listening to the drum beat of your own life. I believe God gives each of us a beat to walk to. My assignment isn't yours and your assignment isn't mine. I am not going to make myself a slave to other human beings. Neither should you! Have friends, have colleagues, have loved ones—but not masters.

STEADY ON

"Each of you should continue to live in whatever situation the Lord has placed you, and remain as you were when God first called you."
1 Corinthians 7:17a

We each have a conscience and we each have to live by it. It is dangerous to ignore your conscience. It is also dangerous to place your conscience in the hands of other people. If you know Jesus, you have a personal relationship with Him. Talk to Him and listen to Him. Tune out the peanut gallery. Everyone has an opinion, but you don't have to live your life by someone else's. Theirs may be a good compass for them; it's a poor one for you. Your compass is inside your soul.

NOVEMBER 5

NOW

"And now we thank you, our God, and praise your glorious name."
1 Chronicles 29:13 (ESV)

Let's circle the word "now." The present. In this moment. It's nice to plan to give God thanks at the end of a great life or on certain occasions. It's even better to do it now. You may be reading this in the morning or at night. Perhaps you're reading it at work or at home, or somewhere in between. Whatever time it is, wherever you are, give Him thanks and praise right now. Bow your head, look up to the sky, or even get on your knees. Thank Him now.

GIVE THANKS

"give thanks in all circumstances; for this is God's will for you in Christ Jesus."
1 Thessalonians 5:18 (NIV)

The verb we start with here is "give." It is assumed we will have thanks or reasons to thank. The instruction is to give them. Not just when everything is going good, but "in all circumstances" we are to give thanks. Indiscriminately, vigorously, enthusiastically to everyone we can. Make a sticky note today that says "THANKS" on it. Place it where you will see it all day long, and give thanks for every circumstance and to every person you encounter.

NOVEMBER 7

ENDURES

"Give thanks to the Lord, for he is good! His faithful love endures forever."
Psalm 107:1

Notice that the "goodness" being talked about here is in regard to His steady love. Sometimes what happens to us doesn't seem good, or the circumstances we are in are clearly not good. Yet His steadfast, faithful, unrelenting love endures forever. That is the surest sign of His goodness. He never gives up on you. Don't give up on yourself. Don't give up on others. He keeps on going and so can you. Love never fails.

THE NAME

"And give thanks for everything to God the Father in the name of our Lord Jesus Christ."
Ephesians 5:20

Jesus Himself taught us to use His name. Today, take a sticky note and write "JESUS" on it. Try to remember to insert Jesus into every conversation you have. If you have something to be thankful for, be thankful in the name of Jesus. There is something powerful about that name. It's like nothing else in the universe. Jesus is at the core of our thankfulness.

NOVEMBER 9

RULE

"And let the peace that comes from Christ rule in your hearts."
Colossians 3:15a

Something is going to rule today. Don't let it be the news cycle. Don't let it be the words or actions of others. Don't let it be yesterday. Let it be the peace of Jesus. Not the peace of financial security or perfect health. Those can go away. Let the peace of Jesus rule in your heart. Someone or something is going to rule and reign there; you want it to be the Prince of Peace.

JESUS

"...do everything in the name of the Lord Jesus, giving thanks to God the Father through him."
Colossians 3:17b (ESV)

As I've said before, this name is the best entrée to the spiritual world ever. It is a calling card that gets you through every door. It is an account that is never empty and a hospital that never closes. Do everything in the name of Jesus: your leisure and your work, your getting up and your winding down. Let Jesus be in every breath. Be aware today. Work on awareness of Him. I think people will sense it in you if you do.

NOVEMBER 11

EVERY

"Every good gift and every perfect gift is from above, coming down from the Father of lights...."
James 1:17a (ESV)

James, brother of Jesus, uses some beautiful prose here. He says every good gift and every perfect gift. We all know there are gifts that are good but not perfect. There are moments when you feel like asking, "God, is that You?" Know in your heart the answer is yes. Every good gift and every perfect gift is from Him. Even if He doesn't sign it with His signature, it's covered with His fingerprints. Look for His fingerprints today.

THANKFULNESS

"Don't worry about anything; instead, pray about everything. Tell God what you need, and thank him for all he has done."
Philippians 4:6

Paul is instructing the early believers that when they are praying in the middle of tough times, they should also insert some thankfulness. Pray about everything. And never pray without at least a little thankfulness. In the middle of a crisis: thankfulness. In the middle of a celebration: thankfulness. When you rise in the morning and when you go to bed at night: thankfulness. Whatever you pray for, insert thanks. I don't know if you need to work on this, but I do. I'm starting today.

NOVEMBER 13

WONDER

"Thank God for this gift too wonderful for words!"
2 Corinthians 9:15

Have you ever been speechless at something's beauty? I have stood at the edge of the Grand Canyon. How can one explain that? I've also seen the Taj Mahal, one of the wonders of the world. It defies description. Here the writer of Corinthians is saying, "Truly, this is an inexpressible gift!" Thankfully, even though we cannot explain this gift, we can enjoy it. Don't try to put words to it today. Simply savor it.

REPEAT

"Praise the Lord! Give thanks to the Lord, for he is good! His faithful love endures forever."
Psalm 106:1

The psalmist repeats himself frequently, especially this refrain. I have referenced it several times throughout the year, most recently in Psalm 107. I repeat it yet again because the psalmist felt it was worthy of repeating. Give thanks! He is good! His love endures forever! Don't pay attention to how you feel. Pay attention to what is real. Really, truly, He is good! Give thanks today.

NOVEMBER 15

GREATNESS

"Give thanks to the Lord and proclaim his greatness. Let the whole world know what he has done."
Psalm 105:1

One of the things we learn about God's greatness is that if He really is all He says He is, we can approach Him. He says to come to Him as a friend. As a Father, even. Yet so many act like they are afraid of Him. Be comfortable coming to God. Thank Him for how good He has been. Talk to Him about what you need, what you hope, and what you wonder. Not just about your dilemmas, but your dreams, too. He is a great listener. Take time to talk to Him today.

FREE

"...and the Lord answered me and set me free."
Psalm 118:5b

I like that. I really like that. God not only answered me, He also set me free. He not only heard you and said yes, He unlocked the jail cell and let you go. Do you believe it, or do you feel and act like you're still stuck behind bars, sentenced with a guilty verdict? How would you act if you really believed you are free? If you knew nothing could be remembered, held, or levied against you? I think you would be a lot more joyful. Live free today.

NOVEMBER 17

REMEMBER

"And always be thankful."
Colossians 3:15b

I like how Scripture is always throwing in thankfulness. The first part of this verse addresses a different topic, but it concludes with the comment, "And always be thankful." In other words, "Don't forget to say thank you." It's like the prompt my grandmother used to give when I would forget to say the words. Whatever today brings, let's remember to be thankful.

YOUR

"May he grant your heart's desires and make all your plans succeed."
Psalm 20:4

Yes, yes, yes! That's my prayer for you today. I am going to insert your name. "May He grant ___________'s heart's desires and fulfill all of ___________'s plans." Insert your own name now and pray it. Then do the same for the people you love.

OUT LOUD

"that I might sing praises to you and not be silent. O Lord my God, I will give you thanks forever!"
Psalm 30:12

There is an old rabbinical proverb that says, "Thankfulness in the heart is not thankfulness." What does that mean? It means you have to say it! Just because it's in your heart doesn't mean it has become real to the rest of us. Don't be silent about God's goodness. Speak it today.

WATCHFUL

"Continue steadfastly in prayer,
being watchful in it with thanksgiving."
Colossians 4:2 (ESV)

I like the idea of being watchful in my prayers. Watching for good things to happen, watching for opportunities. Many people pray like they're throwing a Hail Mary pass in a football game. Instead, let's be steadfast, watchful, and thankful. Maybe even begin a journal today of all of the things you pray and keep it somewhere you can refer to it often. Watch for what happens. I think you will be pleasantly surprised.

NOVEMBER 21

PROTOCOL

"Enter his gates with thanksgiving; go into his courts with praise."
Psalm 100:4a

This is language used for a king. The palace had gates and the king had courts. So this is God's protocol for how He wants to be approached. Enter God's house with thanksgiving and His courts, where the King rules, with praise. Keep that in mind when you want to be in God's presence. Thank and praise. It's His protocol and He is the King.

KNOW

"Yes, they knew God, but they wouldn't worship him as God or even give him thanks."
Romans 1:21a

Having a notion that God exists is not the same thing as knowing God Himself. We all know people by name about whom we don't know any details. Or maybe we've heard or read some information about them, but never met them or built a relationship of any kind. Don't be caught knowing God's name and some things about Him, but not knowing Him personally. There is nothing sadder than having access to greatness but never tapping into it. Find a way to honor God today. Start by giving Him thanks.

NOVEMBER 23

YOU WILL

"In that day you will say:
'Give praise to the Lord….'"
Isaiah 12:4a (NIV)

Isaiah was a prophet. Not only did he predict what God was going to say; he predicted what God's people were going to say. Here Isaiah tells us there will come a day when we are going to give thanks. When we are really going to realize how good God has been to us. Maybe you are already living that day. If you are not, the day will come when you realize you are blessed. I hope it's today.

BY NAME

"I always thank my God when I pray for you, Philemon."
Philemon 1:4

The writer mentions by name the person for whom he thanks God and prays. Who are the key people in your circle? Who are the people who matter most to you on this earth? Say their names out loud this morning as you pray. Thank God that they were put in your world. I'm going to do it. In fact, I'm going to start right now.

NOVEMBER 25

APPROACH

"Let us come to him with thanksgiving.
Let us sing psalms of praise to him."
Psalm 95:2

Remember the thanks + praise combination from Psalm 100? Here it is again. The protocol for entering God's presence is thankfulness. If you can't feel Him, hear Him, or see His work in your life right now, ramp up the gratitude and joy. You don't have to plead for His presence. You can enter His presence with thanksgiving and praise. Turn up the praise music today.

TEST

"'Bring all the tithes into the storehouse so there will be enough food in my Temple. If you do,' says the Lord of Heaven's Armies, 'I will open the windows of heaven for you. I will pour out a blessing so great you won't have enough room to take it in! Try it! Put me to the test!'"
Malachi 3:10

Ponder this today. It may seem counter intuitive, but I have personally experienced it to be true. When you consider all your money to be God's and you give a portion back to Him, it really does open up the windows of heaven. Don't just take my word for it; see for yourself whether this instruction proves as true for you as it has for me. Find someplace you trust, give there generously, and see what happens. I double dare you.

NOVEMBER 27

SUBSTANCE

"Honour the Lord with thy substance, and with the firstfruits of all thine increase."
Proverbs 3:9 (KJV)

Substance is the stuff that makes life happen. It's not about how much you make or have; it's about honoring Jesus with what you have. I often say that I don't believe in a "prosperity gospel;" I believe in a "generosity gospel." I think you can be poor and have the most generous heart in town. And I think you can be rich and give something that seems significant but doesn't really cost you. Think about your generosity today. See if you can contemplate a new goal for the new year that makes more room for God to be honored with your substance, and not just with your words.

FAITH

"And it is impossible to please God without faith."
Hebrews 11:6a

I know we like our facts and variables and plans all lined up before we take a step. But you will find it difficult to have a warm relationship with your Creator if you can't trust Him until you have all the pieces in place. Think about it. When is the last time you had it all lined up (and it actually happened the way you planned)? Life gives us ample opportunities to trust Him; rarely do we have all the details worked out or even within our control. I want Him to be pleased with you. I want Him to be pleased with me. Let's start with trust. What dilemma can you trust Him with today?

NOVEMBER 29

REBUKE

"And I will rebuke the devourer for your sakes..."
Malachi 3:11a (NKJV)

I hardly ever waste my time talking to the devil, but the Bible does give me the authority to do so when I need to. I prefer to talk to my friends and not my enemies. But when I talk to an enemy, I want to have the right words. From Malachi we learn that we can rebuke the devourer. When things are going sideways, spend most of your time talking to Jesus. But if you have to address the devourer, rebuke him in Jesus' name and tell him "hands off my life."

POWER SOURCE

"Remember the Lord your God. He is the one who gives you power to be successful, in order to fulfill the covenant he confirmed to your ancestors with an oath."
Deuteronomy 8:18

Trust me, your strengths are evident to everyone who knows you. You're smart, you're hard working, and you have had experiences other people haven't. So you have every advantage you need for the assignment God has given you. But be careful to remember this: it's God who gives you all of that brilliance as well as the power to use it. As hard as you work, as competent as you are, you still can't do it without Him. May your first words to Him this morning be gratitude for all He has given you to do, and for giving you the power to do it.

DECEMBER

ROLE CALL

"The Lord will conquer your enemies when they attack you."
Deuteronomy 28:7a

I know it's not fun to talk about enemies. It's much more enjoyable to talk about friends. If you have been around very long, you have some of both. Don't worry about revenge. Don't spend your energy contemplating what to do against other people. God keeps good books. He knows your stuff and their stuff. Let Him figure it out. You be a blessing; let God decide what is next for others. This will be hard to do, but restrain yourself today and unleash God.

CATALYST

"You say you have faith, for you believe that there is one God. Good for you! Even the demons believe this, and they tremble in terror."
James 2:19

This explains why Scripture puts so much emphasis on our beliefs not just being an intellectual concept, but also an integrated catalyst reflected in our actions. Am I, are you, doing something about what we believe? Let's each choose one area today and ask Jesus to help us more genuinely apply what we believe to how we live. Work, neighbors, family, friends… I'm starting with work today. How about you?

THREE THINGS

"...teaching in the synagogues and announcing the Good News about the Kingdom. And he healed every kind of disease and illness."
Matthew 9:35b

Jesus was teaching, preaching, and healing. These three things ought to be happening around us all the time. Teaching to increase knowledge and wisdom. People do better when they know better. Preaching to inspire through proclaiming who Jesus is and what the Kingdom is about. Healing for hurt, pain, and sickness. Find and be part of a group of Jesus people who gather around these three things regularly. If you are already connected to a group like this, reach out today to those friends and encourage them.

INWARDLY

"Outwardly you look like righteous people, but inwardly your hearts are filled with hypocrisy and lawlessness."
Matthew 23:28

It's the way of our culture to judge people by their outward appearance. Don't fall into that trap. The way of the Kingdom is to see who people are on the inside. Make sure you are someone who concerns yourself with your own character and forgiveness. That way you push out hypocrisy and rebellion. Work on yourself; you can do that right now. Before you start your day, bow your head and repent, forgive, and move on. You will live more freely, and your day will be different.

SPILLED

"All of us must die eventually. Our lives are like water spilled out on the ground, which cannot be gathered up again."
2 Samuel 14:14a

This is sobering because it is true. Rather than letting this thought bring you down, let it lift you up and shape your outlook today. Life is precious, and you have today. In fact, you have this moment. We can't get it back, so let's make the most of every moment and minute we have. Not sure what to do with a moment in front of you? Ask Jesus. He is with us every step of the way.

DECEMBER 6

SUSTAINED

"You take care of the earth and water it, making it rich and fertile. The river of God has plenty of water; it provides a bountiful harvest of grain, for you have ordered it so."
Psalm 65:9

God has already done His part for you to have a great life today. He has sustained us physically and He has sustained us spiritually. Water is always the picture of abundant life. There are not a lot of things you need for life. The essentials are water, light, and air. Jesus is all of those things to your spirit. He is the way, the truth, and the life. Be aware today of all that happened even before you got up so you could have a great life.

GOOD NEWS

"Good news from far away is like cold water to the thirsty."
Proverbs 25:25

Does it seem to you that we tend to hold on to bad news longer than we do good news? Let's not do that today. Ponder the good news, and since you know it will be welcome, share it with someone else. I believe gossip is the devil's counterfeit for evangelism. Good news is sharing Jesus, who is life; gossip is sharing death. Be a good news person who speaks life today.

DECEMBER 8

LIVING WATER

"Anyone who believes in me may come and drink! For the Scriptures declare, 'Rivers of living water will flow from his heart.'"
John 7:38

It is my goal that people perceive me this way. When I meet new people I can always tell what is bubbling up inside them and flowing from their hearts. For some it is bitterness; for others it is worry or fear. If our meditation and thoughts are on Jesus and His principles, then today somebody will see Him flowing from our hearts.

QUENCHED

"But those who drink the water I give will never be thirsty again. It becomes a fresh, bubbling spring within them."
John 4:14a

Does this mean we will never have needs? No. Does it mean we will never struggle? Certainly not. What it means is that our spiritual need has been quenched. You won't ever need another savior. You won't ever need another cross, crucifixion, or resurrection. He has satisfied the need for retribution. You are free from the inside out. Live like it today.

DECEMBER 10

LISTENING

"Wise words are like deep waters; wisdom flows from the wise like a bubbling brook."
Proverbs 18:4

When you read books about getting along with other people, they almost always tell you to pay closer attention to the people with whom you are conversing. Look them in the eye and listen to their words. When we do this, we not only get closer to people, we find out how deep they really are. What people say when you are listening gives you a window into their soul. If they are hurting, offer them healing. If they are happy, rejoice with them. Listen today. Be a really good listener and slow to speak. This might be hard, but let's try it.

HEADWATERS

"Then the angel showed me a river with the water of life, clear as crystal, flowing from the throne of God and of the Lamb."
Revelation 22:1

Don't avoid the apocalyptic books in your Bible. The apocalypse or revelation simply reveals things that have been happening in the supernatural—things that will become increasingly obvious rather than obscured. This language is meant to give you a picture of your present and your future. Every civilization is built around a river. The church, a gathering of believers, is built around the love and grace that flows from Jesus. Stay close to His love and grace today; it is your source of life.

DECEMBER 12

WILL

"There will be swarms of living things wherever the water of this river flows. Fish will abound in the Dead Sea, for its waters will become fresh. Life will flourish wherever this water flows."
Ezekiel 47:9

This prophesy was given when the nation of Israel was in captivity to their enemies. Ezekiel said over them, "It's going to get better." Let that be the message for you today. You may feel like you're in captivity in one way or another. But it's going to get better. A river is going to run through your dry season. Everything around it will live. It's a Jesus thing.

CLEAN

"Those who suffer from a serious skin disease must tear their clothing and leave their hair uncombed. They must cover their mouth and call out, 'Unclean! Unclean!'"
Leviticus 13:45

These were real lepers and real laws. But Jesus overturned the whole system when He met lepers, touched lepers, and went to the homes of lepers. This world has a way of making us feel "unclean" and trying to make us declare it to everyone around us. But the devil is a liar. If you are a follower of Jesus, you are not unclean; you are forgiven. That is as clean as you can possibly be. Don't go through your day declaring your mistakes. Declare His victory and forgiveness instead.

DECEMBER 14

DISCERNMENT

"Anyone who rebukes a mocker will get an insult in return. Anyone who corrects the wicked will get hurt."
Proverbs 9:7

Have you noticed this? Some people are just so willfully ignorant that they take your correction and advice and turn it into a curse. Learn quickly if someone doesn't receive your blessing or instruction. Move on, friend. You will have a better day and a better life.

WISDOM

"Wisdom will multiply your days
and add years to your life."
Proverbs 9:11

Make this a prayer and ask for it today. If you know someone who is struggling, pray it for them, over them, by name and out loud. Scripture tells us, "If you need wisdom, ask our generous God, and he will give it to you. He will not rebuke you for asking" (James 1:5). Ask for wisdom in Jesus' name, believe you will receive it, and claim the promise that your days and the days of those you pray for will be multiplied and years of life will be added.

SHEPHERD

"The Lord is my shepherd; I have all that I need."
Psalm 23:1

Think for a moment about Jesus as your shepherd. Why do you think the Bible uses this particular role to describe Him? What does a shepherd do? He corrals us. He watches over us. He keeps us moving in the right direction. He leads us to what we need. Keep your eyes and ears open to the Shepherd's leading today.

RESTORER

"He lets me rest in green meadows;
he leads me beside peaceful streams.
He renews my strength."
Psalm 23:2-3a

Jesus gives rest for my body and my mind and then He refreshes me and renews my strength. Get in His presence today. He is rest and renewal in a world that wears and wearies.

DECEMBER 18

LEADER

"He leads me in paths of righteousness for his name's sake."
Psalm 23:3b (ESV)

Jesus leads you to righteousness because there is a bigger storyline going on than yours. He is not trying to help you be pure and righteous so He can steal your fun. He is writing a bigger story of which we are a small part. Today, enjoy your role supporting His lead in the greatest story ever.

EVEN WHEN

"Even when I walk through the darkest valley..."
Psalm 23:4a

The key words here are "even when." These are words of commitment. They say, I know it will not be easy but I am going to do it anyway because it's the right thing, because it is what a great woman or a great man would do. Trust Jesus with your "even when" today.

DECEMBER 20

NOT ALONE

"...I will not be afraid,
for you are close beside me..."
Psalm 23:4b

Evil is something to be afraid of if you are alone. Jesus is someone you want beside you. He is well able to defeat any threat. And if you are His follower, He is close beside you at all times. Are you feeling afraid? You don't need to. Remember He is with you today.

GUARDIAN

"Your rod and your staff protect and comfort me."
Psalm 23:4c

These are typical shepherd's tools used to pull back, prod, and defend. Jesus is doing the same for you and me today.

DECEMBER 22

STRATEGIC JOY

"You prepare a feast for me
in the presence of my enemies."
Psalm 23:5a

Why God does this, I don't know. But He does. He lets us enjoy things while our enemies are watching. Your enemies are bothered by your happiness. They would rather you be miserable. Would you like to defeat your enemies today? Be happy. Sometimes it really is that simple.

HONOR & BLESSING

"You honor me by anointing my head with oil.
My cup overflows with blessings."
Psalm 23:5b

God honors us. He has selected you for greatness and abundant blessing. Wow! Even on our best day we don't come close to being worthy of honor from God Himself. Yet He gives it. Humbling thought, isn't it? Live today remembering you are anointed by God. Honor because you've been honored. Bless because you've been blessed.

DECEMBER 24

SURELY

"Surely your goodness and unfailing love will pursue me all the days of my life, and I will live in the house of the Lord forever."
Psalm 23:6a

Yes, yes, and a thousand times yes! It's not fate that is tracking you down; it is God's goodness and unfailing love. Surely. With certainty. Whatever tough times you are experiencing today, know that God's goodness and unfailing love are close at your heels. The light always overtakes the night.

EVEN MORE

"Jesus replied, 'But even more blessed are all who hear the word of God and put it into practice.'"
Luke 11:28

This is Jesus' response to a woman who said that His mother, Mary, would be blessed because she gave birth to Him. Jesus responded by saying, "Yes, she is blessed. But everyone who follows Me is even more blessed." That's you! Merry Christmas! Jesus was born through a blessed woman. And if you follow Him, you are more blessed than the most singular woman in history. Fabulous! Enjoy every minute of today.

DECEMBER 26

DON'T LET

"Don't let your hearts be troubled."
John 14:1a

Don't let. That means don't give permission. Your heart is not the place for trouble. Don't allow it to come one step closer. Don't welcome it, don't let it enter, don't give it a home. Rebuke it, reject it, push it out in Jesus' name.

TRUST

"Trust in God, and trust also in me."
John 14:1b

The way to keep trouble out is to fill the space with God, with trust in Him. Our one job is to trust. To believe in the One that God the Father sent because He loves us. My heart is not troubled today. Not because there are not things to be troubled about, but because I am too full of belief to let the enemy in.

DECEMBER 28

TOLD

"He has told you, O mortal, what is good; and what does the LORD require of you…?"
Micah 6:8a (NRSV)

Some would like to believe God has not been clear about what He wants from us and for us. The prophet Micah says He has made it obvious. Don't hide behind your ignorance. If you don't know enough about what God wants, look in His word and ask Him personally today.

REQUIRED

"...but to do justice, and to love kindness, and to walk humbly with your God?"
Micah 6:8b

The question here is rhetorical. The writer is saying God has told us these are three things He wants from every person: justice, kindness, and humility in relationship with Him. Justice is how we relate to each other. Kindness is the spirit we have in us and nurture in others. Humility is admitting we are not God and acknowledging the One who is. Work on these three today: justice, kindness, and humility.

TIMING

"The Lord isn't really being slow about his promise...."
2 Peter 3:9a

Just because God doesn't do things on your schedule doesn't mean He is slow. The picture is bigger than we can see. That's why we're not the ones in control of the timeline. Thank God for His timing; if it seems He is being slow, He has a good reason.

ALLEGIANCE

"This is the day the Lord has made."
Psalm 118:24a

Such a simple statement, such a powerful truth. Today is not just the last day of a calendar year. It is the day the Lord has made. Like every day He makes, it is a new day. The Romans used to swear allegiance to the king every New Year's day. Who are you swearing allegiance to today? Let it be Jesus. Happy New Year!

ABOUT THE AUTHOR

Dean Curry is a Jesus guy, husband, father, brother, son, friend, pastor, student, and teacher.

Twitter: @DeanCurry
Instagram: @deancurry
Facebook: @deangcurry